Praise for *Writing with At-Risk Youth*

"Richard Gold's creativity, compassion, and empathy, coupled with his deep sense of the integrity of the human spirit, has allowed healing and restorative expressions to flow from adolescents who have experienced profound emotional traumas. The Pongo Method is essentially a way for these young people—many with severe emotional problems and some who have been ensnared in the juvenile justice system—to learn to communicate and think about their life experience through poetry and storytelling. Many are able to reframe horrific experiences and put some closure around 'issues' that they have held back from feeling and thinking about. Although the Pongo 'process' is not therapy in a traditional sense, it represents the essential elements of the most effective treatments and does this through a modality that youth can engage in with honesty and trust." —**Eric Trupin**, *PhD, professor and vice chair in the Department of Psychiatry and Behavioral Sciences, University of Washington School of Medicine; professor and director of Division of Public and Behavioral Health; director of Evidence Based Practice Institute, Seattle, Washington*

"For even the seasoned teacher, working with traumatized children can be intimidating. *Writing with At-Risk Youth: The Pongo Teen Writing Method* not only inspires teachers to help these youth write poetry but also provides clear instructions on how to facilitate the work—all while taking care of these children. It proves an essential tool for anyone with the heart to take on this important vocation." —**Teri Hein**, *executive director, 826 Seattle, Seattle, Washington*

"*Writing with At-Risk Youth* is a step-by-step guide in understanding the minds of at-risk youth. By following a carefully planned writing program, the guide helps the instructor liberate youth from past trauma. The road to recovery is bumpy, but this guide can make their journey smoother." —**Charles Shelan**, *CEO, Community Youth Services, Olympia, Washington*

"I have had the pleasure of working with and learning from Gold, with his remarkably creative and effective method, in our work together with incarcerated youth and adults. He is a superb clinician and teacher, and I recommend this unique book, *Writing with At-Risk Youth*, to anyone who chooses to work with this underserved population." —**E. K. Rynearson**, MD, *clinical professor of psychiatry, University of Washington School of Medicine, Seattle, Washington*

"For many years as an incarcerated youth, writing was my principal method of venting in a highly constrained and rule-governed environment, and now as an adult working with incarcerated youth it is more clear to me than ever how powerful a tool writing can be for youth going through that experience. . . . By the time I reached the end of the book I was convinced of the potential for empowerment that can come from *Writing with At-Risk Youth*. That marvelous poetry is there locked inside these troubled youth; the method is clearly effective in helping them bring it to the world." —**Starcia Ague**, *program coordinator, University of Washington, Division of Public Behavioral Health and Justice Policy, Seattle, Washington*

"In *Writing with At-Risk Youth*, Gold takes on the incredible task of demystifying the teaching of poetry for at-risk youth. The book is a straightforward, beautiful, and heartfelt how-to for educators of any age . . . and a testament to the compassionate tools Gold employs in his own teaching approach, as well as the tenderness he feels toward emotionally troubled youth." —**Pat Graney**, *founder, Keeping the Faith/The Prison Project, Seattle, Washington*

"'[T]he world of Pongo poetry,' writes author Richard Gold, 'is about . . . tuning into an underground river of unarticulated emotion, that rumbles and roars just beneath the surface of our world. We can feel it through the soles of our feet, when we attend to it, and it shakes us.' In these pages Gold carries the reader deftly into this subterranean realm, in which carefully crafted expressive writing provides soundings from the hearts of troubled teens who are helped to write with startling depth and honesty. By following the Pongo model, writing mentors and counselors can help young people hear and share their own emotional truths, and participate in the seismic shifts they foster." —**Robert A. Neimeyer**, PhD, *editor of* Grief and the Expressive Arts: Practices for Creating Meaning; *professor, University of Memphis, Memphis, Tennessee*

"*Writing with At-Risk Youth* makes a wonderful contribution to our collective response to youth affected by trauma and hardship. Facing up to trauma experiences and developing a new narrative is proven to work for recovery. Expressive writing is an amazingly powerful method of doing just that. This book helps youth to find their voice, learn their strengths, and give themselves hope for their future." —**Lucy Berliner**, *MSW; director, Harborview Center for Sexual Assault and Traumatic Stress; clinical associate professor, University of Washington School of Social Work and Department of Psychiatry and Behavioral Sciences, Seattle, Washington*

"*Writing with At-Risk Youth* collects Gold's more than twenty years spent working with troubled youth. In it I hear his voice and everything he told me when I volunteered for him as a writing mentor in Seattle's juvenile detention. This book is a clear guide on how to apply his expressive writing methods in any setting, but his thoughts and stories about the work remind us how transformational it can be for young people who need this empowerment the most. For my own trauma-serving poetry project in Sacramento, founded with Gold's guidance, this book will be required reading for all of my future poet mentors." —**Alex Russell**, *founder, Real Poets Writing Project, Sacramento, California*

"Sadly, the juvenile justice system has become the dumping ground for youth who have mental health issues or a history of trauma or both. All incarcerated youth are suffering. That suffering will find expression: positive or negative. *Writing with At-Risk Youth* is a user-friendly book that offers a pro-social, holistic, and low-cost solution." —**Will Harrell**, *ombudsman, Youth Studies Center (detention center), New Orleans, Louisiana*

"On its surface *Writing with At-Risk Youth: The Pongo Teen Writing Method* is a how-to manual for designing and delivering a program that uses poetry to draw out, expose, and confront its young authors' demons, and open the path to their redemption. Through their profoundly moving poems and the heartbreaking backstories that Gold tells, you find yourself walking alongside these young poets, sharing their pain, informed by their revelations, and inspired by their resiliency. You soon realize, this book is much more than just an instructional guide. It's an homage to poetry itself and a testament to its healing power." —**David Nollman**, *program coordinator, Club Z In-Home Tutoring, Boston, Massachusetts*

Writing with
At-Risk Youth

Also in the It's Easy to W.R.I.T.E. Expressive Writing Series

Expressive Writing: Foundations of Practice
Edited by Kathleen Adams

The Flourishing Principal: Strategies for Self-Renewal
Kathleen Adams and Rosemary Lohndorf

The Teacher's Journal: A Workbook for Self-Discovery
Kathleen Adams and Marisé Barreiro

Writing with At-Risk Youth

The Pongo Teen Writing Method

RICHARD GOLD

ROWMAN & LITTLEFIELD EDUCATION
A Division of
ROWMAN & LITTLEFIELD
Lanham • Boulder • New York • Toronto • Plymouth, UK

Published by Rowman & Littlefield Education
A division of Rowman & Littlefield
4501 Forbes Boulevard, Suite 200, Lanham, Maryland 20706
www.rowman.com

10 Thornbury Road, Plymouth PL6 7PP, United Kingdom

British Library Cataloguing in Publication Information Available

Library of Congress Cataloging-in-Publication Data
Gold, Richard, 1948–
  Writing with at-risk youth : the Pongo teen writing method / Richard Gold.
    pages cm. — (It's easy to W.R.I.T.E expressive writing series)
  Includes bibliographical references.
  ISBN 978-1-4758-0283-2 (cloth : alk. paper)—ISBN 978-1-4758-0284-9 (pbk. : alk. paper)— ISBN 978-1-4758-0285-6 (electronic)
  1. Teenagers with social disabilities—Education. 2. Creative writing (Secondary education). I. Title.
  LC4085.G65 2014
  371.826'94—dc23   2013044051

∞™ The paper used in this publication meets the minimum requirements of American National Standard for Information Sciences—Permanence of Paper for Printed Library Materials, ANSI/NISO Z39.48-1992.

Printed in the United States of America

Contents

Series Overview: About the *It's Easy to W.R.I.T.E.* Expressive Writing Series

Expressive writing originates from the writer's lived experience—past, present, or imagined future life. Written in the author's own voice, expressive writing creates bridges between thought and feeling, reason and intuition, idea and action. It is equally rooted in language arts and social science, and it takes multiple forms: journals, poetry, life story, personal essay, creative nonfiction, song lyrics, notes, and snippets of thought. Expressive writing is democratic and accessible. No special knowledge is needed, supplies are available and affordable, and research confirms that outcomes can be profound and even life-changing.

The *It's Easy to W.R.I.T.E.* Expressive Writing Series captures the voices of worldwide experts on the power of writing for personal development, academic improvement, and lasting behavioral change. Authors are both theorists and practitioners of the work they document, bringing real-life examples of practical techniques and stories of actual outcomes.

Individually or as a compendium, the volumes in the *It's Easy to W.R.I.T.E.* Expressive Writing Series represent thoughtful, innovative, demonstrated approaches to the myriad ways life-based writing can shape both critical thinking and emotional intelligence. Books in the series are designed to have versatile appeal for classroom teachers and administrators, health and behavioral health professionals, graduate programs that prepare educators and counselors, facilitators of expressive writing, and individuals who themselves write expressively. Workbooks offer well-crafted, self-paced writing programs for individual users, with facilitation guides and curricula for anyone who wishes to organize peer-writing circles to explore the material in community.

Each book or chapter author is held to exacting standards set by the series editor, Kathleen Adams, who, prior to her 1985 launch as a pioneer and global expert in the expressive writing field, was trained as a journalist and served as chief editor for a nonfiction publishing company.

It's Easy to W.R.I.T.E.

*W*hat do you want to write about? Name it. Write it down. (If you don't know, try one of these: *What's going on? How do I feel? What's on my mind? What do I want? What's the most important thing to do? What's the best/worst thing right now?*)

*R*econnect with your center. Close your eyes. Take three deep breaths. Focus. Relax your body and mind. Gather your thoughts, feelings, questions, ideas.

*I*nvestigate your thoughts and feelings. Start writing and keep writing. Follow the pen/keyboard. If you get stuck, close your eyes and recenter yourself. Reread what you've already written and continue. Try not to edit as you go; that can come later, if at all.

*T*ime yourself. Write for five to twenty minutes or whatever time you choose. Set the timer on your phone, stove, or computer. Plan another three to five minutes at the end for reflection.

*E*xit smart. Reread what you've written and reflect on it in a sentence or two: *As I read this, I notice . . .* or *I'm aware of . . .* or *I feel . . .* Note any action steps you might take or any prompts you might use for additional writes.

Foreword

In our worlds as teachers, counselors, health care givers, parents, comrades—fellow human beings—how do we learn to be helpers? How do we help struggling young folks develop the voice and power to share their stories, hopes, and fears in a way that helps them have a rising sense of optimism and a positive purpose along the way?

Surely it is a two-way street. As a physician for thirty-three years, I have long since realized that I, and we in the helper guilds, are ever the students of life. The youth who have written for Pongo, at the hospital where I am an attending psychiatrist, have joined the pantheon of teachers for me. They are stronger from writing and sharing; they have new tools now to help themselves. They can find an enthusiasm that is contagious. The youth and their poetry have enlivened and deepened my work.

Two years ago a fifteen-year-old patient, who had a Pongo mentor in the preceding year, caught me in the hall at school to share a reflection he had written that morning in class. This is a young man who knows recurrent sorrow, deep self-doubt, and a still-overwhelming, flawed struggle to do right and good.

Som times I Fiel Like A Peney (the youth's original title)
by a young man in the state psychiatric hospital, age 15

I feel like a penny,
Alone,
Thrown away.
My body ain't worth a penny.
I feel like a lost lonely penny.
No one cares about a penny.
Pennies are all being thrown away.
Pennies are not used very often.

I feel like I've just been abandoned by my friend.
People are throwing pennies away saying that they aren't worth much,
    That they are garbage.

There I lay in the dark,
    Waiting to be picked up,
    Lying there helpless, motionless.
Pennies are being thrown away and not being used.

I wait to be used, I wait to be worth something, I wait to be helpful now,
    Maybe help kids that have diseases.
I could be worth something.
Now.
I can be helpful.

The quest to be useful for our students and patients is often daunting, mystifying, and painful. My young man's musings have been a touchstone for me in the intervening seasons, as have many of his fellow writers' offerings.

It is now over twenty years that I have served as a psychiatrist in a state long-term psychiatric hospital program, serving children from the ages of five to seventeen years. Our hospital is, at once, a refuge and an exile zone, a place to be safe and also a place for painful work. I have longed, for years, to weave together treatment strategies that can help our kids find coherence and strength in their own voices and an enhanced sense of belonging and hope for productivity in the world.

I was delighted when, thirteen years ago, Richard Gold and his team of mentors brought their writing workshops to our program. But I was not prepared for the gifts that seemed to immediately unfold for our young residents. At his first meeting with us, within fifteen minutes, Richard had several dozen usually loud, demanding, and wiggly youth busily writing (or quietly dictating to their counselors and teachers) life-narrative poetry. In another fifteen minutes, the youth were reading their words to each other with more mutual support than I had ever seen from them. I was equally impressed with how Richard helped all of us restless and busy teachers, counselors, and doctors to settle into a mode of mutual support and group productivity that I have rarely seen in hospitals.

Richard has a genius for helping the deep hopes, worries, and confusions of youth safely make it into poetry. He is perhaps to be most commended for his painstaking and fruitful efforts to distill for his readers (and writers) methods that are now accessible to all of us. The evolution of the Pongo Teen Writing website is living proof of that. I am delighted that we now have a close-at-hand manual that has the coherence, depth, breadth, and organization ready made for those of us who are eager for the access and camaraderie that Pongo methods bring. Quite simply, through their earnest and heartfelt narratives, our youth have much to give to themselves and the rest of the world.

Pongo has helped our youth to tell the world their own splendid (though often pained and painful to hear) yearnings. The fields of child and adolescent psychiatry and juvenile justice need Richard Gold and the Pongo Project's careful teachings to be shared. We need the illuminations of youth writing to serve more of us at one time. Pongo's strategies, techniques, and ways of connecting with young people offer remarkable complementarity with the last decade's promising advances in evidence-based psychotherapies for children and adolescents. As a physician, I am better able to be a coinvestigator with my patients when the Pongo approaches are employed. As a physician-educator, I find myself drawing on my patients' poems and expressive narratives to help share constructs on diagnosis, formulation, illness explanation, healing, enhanced patient efficacy, and ways of fostering hope.

No doubt teachers, principals, and other educators will find the same opportunities, through Pongo techniques, for helping youth, for learning from youth, and for inspiring their own professional methods and meaning.

The writings of youth from their Pongo poetry sessions form some of my most treasured vignettes to help illustrate possibilities for young people striving to grow beyond their isolation, trauma, sense of limitations, and sadness into more fulfilling and optimistic lives.

Six months after I had last seen the young man who wrote about feeling like a penny, I was walking with a medical student. We were discussing some of my lessons from caring for the youth when I saw, in the corner of my vision, a penny on the ground. I picked it up, and I have it in a safe but visible (and useful) place on my desk. The penny was a wheat penny from 1953, my birth year. I couldn't wait to tell this young man of my find, and to urge him onward.

Michael (Mick) Storck, MD
Associate Professor
Department of Psychiatry and Behavioral Sciences
University of Washington School of Medicine

Preface

Thank you, teachers and counselors, for all you do to help struggling young people. Thank you for your passion and caring.

You help youth adapt, learn, and grow in the midst of difficult lives. You enjoy the teens' energy and independence, and you are moved and attracted by their vulnerability. You work to make a difference.

But sometimes you may wish you could do more. You may regret the fact that many teens are caught in patterns of self-destructive behavior. You may wish that you could break through the teens' habits of mistrust and isolation. Sometimes, you may feel helpless or sad.

Also, you may have a sense about the potential value of teaching expressive writing in your work, which brought you here, but you may feel unclear where to begin.

This book describes a specific program for teaching and mentoring expressive writing by at-risk youth—a program that can generate transformative change in the teens, and generate significant new satisfactions for you.

When young people write personally and creatively, it helps them to overcome challenges in their lives. They feel better, think more clearly, are more self-confident, and are better able to relate to others, including their helpers. This personal creative process is enriching and enlivening for everyone. It brings emotional clarity and meaning to everyone. It brings closeness, in addition to learning and growth.

Welcome to the Pongo Teen Writing Method.

Who This Book Is For

This book is for anyone who wants to bring expressive writing to young people who've led difficult lives, to offer a range of emotional, relational, educational, and therapeutic benefits. The techniques in this book will help you teach writing to youth either one-on-one or in groups. You may be a special education teacher, a writer who wants to start a poetry program in a prison, a caseworker with homeless youth, the leader of a therapy group for trauma victims, a child therapist, a teacher who wants to start a poetry program in an alternative school, a health care worker. You may also be a professor or mentor of new teachers and counselors, who wants to teach new professionals how to be emotionally open in their work. Through poetry, new teachers and counselors can acquire not only an effective way to help youth, but also an effective way to learn from youth.

What You Will Learn

This book will teach you specific techniques for mentoring writing by youth. It makes no assumptions about the knowledge or experience you bring to this work to start, yet it presents a method that is new, emotionally deep, and subtle. It helps you understand the teens' emotional struggles after trauma, teaches you how to be with them in a helpful and supportive way to encourage writing, explains the particular benefits of poetry, and provides the skills for facilitating poetry. It tells you exactly what to say to new young writers. It tells you how to organize a writing session, including a session in an institutional environment. It gives you writing activities to use.

In addition, the book tells you how to start and organize a new and independent writing project in a school, agency, or institutional setting. It tells you the important issues for keeping everyone safe. It explains the legal issues in publishing a book of teen poetry.

Why This Book Is Unique

This book is unique because it is based on the work of the Pongo Teen Writing Project that has served six thousand youth over seventeen years. Pongo facilitates therapeutic personal poetry by youth in institutional settings, such as juvenile detention and a state psychiatric hospital. The consistent theme in our authors' writing is early childhood trauma. Our particular focus is on individual writers who have a hard time expressing themselves. Pongo's history and outcomes, including research, are explained in the book, to provide context for the techniques we teach.

In addition, Pongo has not only run its own projects, but it has taught hundreds of people the Pongo Teen Writing Method and has mentored highly successful writing projects by others on the Pongo model (called "duckling" projects). The information in this book has not only been used by Pongo for over seventeen years, but it has been communicated successfully to people like you.

How This Book Is Organized

You'll see in the table of contents that this book has fifteen chapters, and they proceed in a logical sequence. The book begins by explaining the emotional and intellectual context for the work, with chapters like "Childhood Trauma and the Benefits of Writing" (chapter 1), "The Special Role of the Writing Mentor" (chapter 3), and "The Pongo Approach to Teaching Poetry" (chapter 5). It continues by explaining the structure of an independent poetry project, with chapters like "A Model Pongo Writing Project" (chapter 6) and "Keeping Everyone Safe" (chapter 7).

The book then explains techniques that are general to teaching poetry and also specific to either one-on-one work or group work with youth. Some examples of these chapters are "Introducing Poetry to Youth" (chapter 8), "Overview of the One-on-One Process" (chapter 9), and "The Challenges of Group Process" (chapter 14).

Where You Can Find Additional Support

One advantage of this book is that Pongo's support for you doesn't end here. The Pongo website contains teen poetry, fifty writing activities, additional information on Pongo techniques, a blog, and more. Pongo invites you to contact us through our website. We offer trainings. We offer free phone consultation to people who are using the Pongo Teen Writing Method and who are starting writing projects on the Pongo model. We would like to offer you a Pongo community.

With Gratitude

I will end this preface on a personal note.

The Pongo work is profound. I have learned universal lessons from witnessing the suffering and resilience of young people. I have learned from them about the deep need to love, the terrible inclination to self-blame, the importance of articulating and sharing one's story, and the power of helping others. I have been helped to find meaning in my life. I am continuing to learn from the Pongo authors after all these years. I dedicate this book to them.

I am also grateful to the Pongo leaders (including Ann Teplick, Adrienne Johanson, and Eli Hastings) and the Pongo volunteer writing mentors. We have all grown together as we shared this experience. It has been a special reward of this work to know them and to feel joy in their life accomplishments.

I wish to thank the Pongo advisors who have helped me to understand the importance of this work, as well as to develop this program. It's an honor to have the support of these individuals. Pongo's advisors include Dr. Mick Storck, Dr. Ted Rynearson, Dr. Eric Trupin, and Dr. Lane Gerber.

I wish to thank Pongo's collaborators at all of the Pongo sites, including the administrators and staff at King County juvenile detention and Child Study and Treatment Center. I wish to thank the Seattle and Clover Park school staff and King County library staff at those sites.

I wish to thank Pongo's many grantors, supporters, and friends, whose kindnesses have been a wonderful encouragement over the years. I'd like to particularly acknowledge the significant contributions of Pongo's web designer, Yasmine Rafii of Y Art Works, and Pongo's attorney, Robert C. Cumbow of Graham&Dunn PC.

Finally, on the most personal note, I also dedicate this book to Celeste—my wife, friend, and partner.

Richard Gold
2014

1

Childhood Trauma and the Benefits of Writing

The New Park
by a young man in the state psychiatric hospital, age 12

You're in the park
It's been deserted for many years
Because people have died there
There's a swing set, a slide, monkey bars
And a gymnasium
They're all taken down
They look like a pile of wood
That people loved so much

You start grabbing pieces of wood
You take a hammer and nails
You start to pound the wood together
And you build
A swing set, a tree house
You start to paint
Paint the swing set red
And you paint the tree house
A beautiful red and blue

Blue is because of the sadness
That you had in your life

Then you get a megaphone
And say
That there's a new park
Kids start rushing in
They get on the swing set
And push each other
They look like a heart when they're swinging
They beat

This book, *Writing with At-Risk Youth,* is based on the longtime work of the Pongo Teen Writing Project. Pongo teaches and mentors personal poetry by distressed teens, especially those who have a hard time expressing themselves. It runs writing projects inside juvenile detention centers, homeless shelters, psychiatric hospitals, and other sites. Pongo has worked with six thousand youth over seventeen years. The consistent theme in our authors' poetry is childhood trauma, such as abuse and neglect.

Trauma is the terrible reality of many teens' lives. Trauma is an overwhelming hurtful experience that alters a young person's emotional universe (Herman 1997, van der Kolk 2007b, Kalsched 2001). Many teens are referred to as "at risk" because they engage in behavior that jeopardizes their success and happiness. Many are referred to as "at risk" because they come from circumstances of poverty, lack of education, and substance abuse that are seen as precursors of this behavior. *This book, to explain the purposes and methods of expressive writing, discusses struggling youth not in terms of their behavior but in terms of their distress, and in particular their distress after trauma.*

The depth and constancy of the teens' pain, and their sense of damage, pose a great challenge to them, one that profoundly affects their teachers and counselors, too. There is often helplessness and sadness all around.

Expressive writing—authentic expression of a teen's lived experience—can make a tremendous difference for distressed youth, and for the adults who work with them. Expressive writing can engage teens constructively, in a *transformative way,* in their lives; it can also bring additional satisfaction and meaning to the work of the helping professionals who share their world.

Expressive writing can enliven schools and agencies and make important and hopeful differences in society. The ways of expressive writing, as described in the Pongo Teen Writing Method, are simple, and they work.

This transformation is symbolized in the opening poem, "The New Park," which was written by a twelve-year-old boy in the Washington State psychiatric hospital for children. This boy had suffered from near-fatal cancer, but was saved by a transplant. A dead part of himself was replaced by a living part.

At the beginning of the boy's poem he describes an old park, which is dead, a pile of rubble, deserted after people have died there. But with determination, the poet reconstructs this park he once loved. Part of the new park is painted blue, honoring an enduring sadness, but the park is built with a vital core. *All* children are called to play there, where red swings beat like a heart.

Through expressive writing, pain and sadness can be part of a process of emotional honesty that leads to growth for everyone, teens and adults—a reconstructive process that includes prideful resilience and a great deal of joy.

Cherie's Story

What one learns quickly in the Pongo experience is that words like "abuse" and "neglect" are incapable of conveying the nature of our authors' experiences—traumatic experiences that include overwhelming terror, a sense of awful defectiveness, terrible shame, and the feeling of personal responsibility (Herman 1997, van der Kolk 2007b). Words like "abuse" and "neglect" do not necessarily imply the way trauma perseveres inside a person, perhaps for a great many years afterward, through an enduringly devastated and terrorized part of oneself, a part of oneself that may not be consciously understood or even known (Herman 1997, van der Kolk 2007b, Kalsched 2001). Ultimately, what we see in distressed young people, as in many sufferers, is that they adapt to their pain by protecting themselves in the best ways they can. These adaptations are sometimes not constructive and can actually be very hurtful (Herman 1997, van der Kolk 2007b).

In terms of understanding trauma, the poem "The Other Piece of Me, My Father" is one girl's story that illustrates some of trauma's aspects and effect.

The Other Piece of Me, My Father
by a young woman in juvenile detention, age 13

He was a nice person,
but he had problems

He really disappointed me when
he had said, "Don't come home.
No matter what you do, don't come home."
I didn't go home, I was stranded at school
And the lady who lived down the street
had taken me to her house

The next day, I went back home,
and the house was empty, except for my room
I didn't go back to that lady's house,
I stayed at my house by myself
My dad left me money
He left me a portfolio in his room,
next to the telephone,
that had my baby pictures, my birth certificate,
little things that I had given him when I was younger,
and a letter to me, saying
I don't mean to hurt your feelings,
but I care for you a lot,
and I'm sorry that I couldn't be there,
to take care of you,
and I love you very deeply,
and I hope one day you can forgive me.

That's the letter, I was 11

I stayed in the house, by myself,
until the landlord came and kicked me out
So I went back to that lady's house,

and I stayed there for about three months
and then went back to group homes

That's what I get for being a bad kid, I guess
But when people neglect you and abandon you,
it's hard to treat them with respect

Dedicated to my father

I met Cherie in juvenile detention when I took her out of a class to write poetry with me. She was thirteen, but looked younger. Her face and body were round and babyish. Her blond hair was braided in cornrows. In the classroom, as I talked to Cherie, the other girls, who were bigger and older, mocked and snickered at her.

I took Cherie to another room, where I proceeded to take dictation, asking her to tell me what was on her mind. She began by talking about her dad: "He was a nice person, but he had problems." And I couldn't know where her poem was headed. She took a long time to describe, with my questions and help, all that had happened to her one night when her father told her not to come home, all the confusion she experienced because she had nowhere to go. It was a shock for me to hear, finally, that when Cherie did arrive back home in the morning, her father, who was her only parent, had moved out.

How can a single word convey Cherie's experience at the moment of discovering her abandonment? The impact of trauma is overwhelming, yet often inarticulate (van der Kolk 2007b)—like a silent scream that fills a child's mind and body, and continues constantly or periodically, perhaps in the background of life, perhaps forever.

The most telling details in Cherie's poem are that her father left behind her birth certificate and the "little things" she had made for him when she was younger. In this way he seemed to deny his status as her parent. Cherie lost much more than a caretaker, though that would have been terrible enough. Cherie lost the relationship that defines comfort, that provides the structure and encouragement necessary to validate a child's very existence (Herman 1997, van der Kolk 2007b). Imagine the horror for Cherie, how she must have felt emptied of her vital self.

Cherie's poem illustrates another aspect of the trauma of childhood abuse and neglect: The hurt often happens in the context of love, a love made more intense in abusive circumstances (Herman 1997, van der Kolk 2007b, Karen 1998, Davies and Frawley 1994). While we talked, Cherie discussed her dad's behavior with reluctance. She not only began her writing by saying her dad was a nice person, but she ended by dedicating her poem to her dad. It's very common for Pongo's authors to dedicate their poems in this way, without irony or criticism. For Cherie, she was not only denied an essential validation of her life when her father walked out, but she experienced this denial in the context of an enduring love for the person who abandoned her.

A third aspect of trauma that Cherie's poem illustrates is her damaged view of herself. In dictating the story of her abandonment by her father, Cherie's original ending was "That's what I get for being a bad kid, I guess." She felt defective, and she felt deserving of, and even responsible for, the terrible things that have happened to her.

When Cherie first dictated "That's what I get for being a bad kid, I guess," I told her that her ending was a good ending, but I wondered if she had other things to add. At that point she told me about another event in her life. Her mother had abandoned her when Cherie was an infant. She was an angry child. Cherie had been in an anger management class at age eight, and had knocked out the teacher with a chair. Cherie was suffering deeply from multiple traumas, which is typical of Pongo's authors. After our discussion, Cherie went on to create her current ending:

That's what I get for being a bad kid, I guess
But when people neglect you and abandon you,
it's hard to treat them with respect

In this ending we see not only Cherie's suffering, but also how she is served by writing. Cherie told me this was the first time she had talked about what happened to her (something Pongo often hears). The creative experience enabled her to describe an event that was filled with hurt and shame and therefore hard to articulate. In describing the event, however, she could objectify it and relieve some of its pain. The creative experience also enabled her to incorporate complexity into that description, including two conditions that were difficult for Cherie to accept: that her father was imperfect, though she loved him; and that she might have valid reasons to feel angry, in spite of the fact that she feels defective.

It can easily be missed, in responding as a reader to Cherie's horrible experience, that she is more than a mere victim. Consider the resilience that Cherie showed at eleven years old when she found a place to stay and when she lived on her own. Consider the courage in Cherie's ability to express herself, and grow, through her poem.

When I returned to the classroom with Cherie, she gave me permission to read her poem aloud to the group. The bigger, older girls who had mocked Cherie before, now applauded her. They stood up, hugged her, and patted her on the back, while Cherie beamed.

Trauma and Fragmentation

As shown in Cherie's story, the effects of trauma are extremely complicated and difficult to describe. For example, how does a young person even contemplate a parent's hurtful actions? How does a young person reconcile those actions with the need for love? How does a young person accept the validity of her feelings, such as anger, when those same feelings are felt to be the product of her own defectiveness?

And how does a young person feel about surviving, much less thriving, when the people she loves don't care?

Ultimately, someone like Cherie feels all of these things at the same time and separately. A person is fragmented by trauma (Herman 1997, Davies and Frawley 1994). Fragmentation is the most confusing outcome of trauma, both for the victim and for the people who care about her. And fragmentation is much more complicated even than the conflicted feelings described above. It includes *separated* experiences of memory and feeling that result in confusion and inexplicable behavior (Herman 1997, van der Kolk 2007b, van der Kolk 2007c, Davies and Frawley 1994).

Imagine that a person sometimes remembers a traumatic event and sometimes does not. Imagine that this same person sometimes feels terror, without knowing why, and sometimes feels numb, or perhaps overtaken by uncontrollable anger, without understanding the cause. Imagine she sometimes acts brilliantly to survive (Herman 1997, van der Kolk 2007b), but at other times recreates trauma, perhaps by forming relationships with people who abuse her (Herman 1997, van der Kolk 2007b).

This fragmentation is the product of being overwhelmed by terrible events, and, in part, the cause is biological (van der Kolk 2007a). Terror can make changes in a person's mind and body. But beyond this biological nature, we can also view fragmentation as one way to survive: Fragmentation disconnects a person from some of her hurt (though it exposes her to hurt, as well) (Herman 1997, van der Kolk 2007b, Kalsched 2001).

For those of us who care about Cherie and young people like her, it means that some of our efforts to help might be disappointing. Sometimes the fragmented pieces of traumatized youth are like shy, transmuting birds that change and fly away as we approach.

But this condition does explain some of the promise in expressive writing. When young people describe their experiences through their writing, those experiences are externalized, separated from some of the internal processes, such as feeling overwhelmed, that make memories threatening and that cause our bird to fly. Also, in expressive writing a person's feelings are expressed and associated with her experience, an important change that helps a young person evolve as an integrated whole. This integration, the connection between "what happened" and "how it affected me," creates an acceptable self-portrait of "This is who I am," and the bird can more easily hold her ground while others approach.

Expressive writing, especially evident in the images and devices of poetry, allows incorporation of complex feelings. For example, a simile such as "love is like drowning" expresses a condition that honors the centrality of both love and its pain. There is relief and transformation in understanding a complicated truth.

Trauma and Low Self-Esteem

In addition to fragmentation, there is another horrible effect of trauma that writing can ameliorate—the teens' low self-esteem. Within Cherie's story, her sense of defectiveness and her burden of shame are an intimate part of the conflicts and states of trauma.

Children need their parents, and their need is deeper than the need for physical care (Herman 1997). Children need their parents to provide an essential sense of who the children are (Karen 1998). Children will automatically go to any lengths to preserve this kernel of identity. When parents disappoint their children deeply, as happens with abuse and neglect, the children feel broken. They feel that they themselves are fundamentally bad. In these circumstances it is easier for children to see themselves as bad than it is for them to see their parents as less than good, as less than good representations of what the children need to be (Herman 1997, van der Kolk 2007b).

For abused and neglected youth, a sense of personal defectiveness is a profound accompaniment to their childhood trauma. Deep shame is another outcome of this disappointment. Youth not only feel flawed after abuse and neglect, they feel repulsive, perhaps worthy of annihilation. They feel less than human (Karen 1998).

A child's sense of badness is further worsened by the blame that is a significant aspect of child abuse (Herman 1997). The perpetrators, and their accomplices, frequently blame the victims for the abuse. One young man in detention started a poem by expressing the belief that, if you want your parents to be good to you, you have to be good to them. When I asked him to explain, he told me how his mother had given him the choice to live with his aunt when he was seven. When he made that choice, his mom used the boy's decision as an excuse to reject him forever and never speak to him again. The mom made the boy take responsibility for her rejection of him.

As another example, one girl in juvenile detention wrote a poem about how her mother's boyfriend raped her repeatedly when she was ten years old. He planned these rapes. The girl watched him getting her mother drunk, and knew what would follow. But when the brave girl was able to tell her mother what was happening, her mother blamed the girl for wearing seductive shorts.

Of course these children—who feel defective, ashamed, and blamed—are only more deeply confirmed in their negative self-image when their understandable confusion and hurt sometimes manifest themselves in struggles with school, behavioral problems, dependence on drugs, involvement in the justice and/or mental health systems, flawed relationships, and other difficulties.

Yet, even though traumatized youth may suffer a sense of defectiveness, shame, and blame, there is hope in the transformative possibility of expressive writing. Not only does expressive writing integrate a fragmented world by articulating and connecting experience and feeling, but expressive writing can also substantiate a child's unique identity and sense of a good self. For children who write expressively, they not only benefit from an integrative understanding of "This is who I am," but they benefit from the very act of making that declaration.

Children who have been hurt can find their voice through poetry, an appropriate assertion of self whose benefit is multiplied by the concrete, external product of a poem. A true, honest, and personal creative outcome is always experienced as a good thing by Pongo's authors, a unique representation of a real and worthy human being. When abused and neglected children write expressively, they create not just poems but themselves.

Trauma and Difficulties with Trust

Caring adults can have a wonderful impact on many distressed teens. But teachers and counselors often feel how hard it is to bridge the distance between themselves and distressed youth, to establish a trusting relationship.

We can understand that, in part, youth are isolated by their fragmented inner world, where they protect themselves behind barriers of confusion. We can understand that, in part, youth are withdrawn from others because they have a horrible view of their own worth.

We can also consider, specifically, the meaning of relationships in the lives of distressed youth. If a parent is abusive or neglectful, a young person may feel betrayed by this most important person in his life, which would seem like reason enough for the child not to trust other people (Herman 1997, van der Kolk 2007b). As with so many aspects of trauma, the nature of relationships for distressed youth is much more complicated.

When one considers young people's love for parents and their wish to preserve these relationships, including their need to believe that their parents are good, a relationship with another person may have unwelcome significance.

Within abusive family systems, young people may carry a lot of responsibility to protect their parents and siblings. They may feel the need to keep the family's secrets, for both external and internal reasons. Young people both idealize their parents and understand their parents' weaknesses. In many cases, victims of abuse accept a role to take care of their abusers emotionally (Schultz 1990). In this role, the victim accepts her victimhood. In addition, the victim may be taking care of not only the abuser but a passive second parent, perhaps, who enables the family's abusive conditions (Schultz 1990, Davies and Frawley 1994). Also, the victim may be doing her best to shield her siblings from unwanted attention and harm. For many reasons, then, a young person's relationships outside the family, including relationships with teachers and counselors, can feel like an intimate betrayal of the people she loves.

Here we see another value of expressive writing. When a teacher or counselor encourages expressive writing, the writing itself exists as an intermediary object between the adult and the child. A poem creates neutral ground on which to relate. It's as if two strangers meet by admiring and petting a puppy. Instead of building a relationship on the basis of liking or trusting one another, with all of the pressures that entails, an adult and child can build a relationship that feels safe for a child when they both like the child's personal writing.

A relationship built in this way is a step toward better future relationships, has important transitional significance, and can carry deep and transformative value for a distressed youth.

The Particular Benefits of Poetry

This chapter has discussed some of the benefits of expressive writing for youth after childhood trauma. Pongo Teen Writing finds very particular benefits to writing poetry, as the expressive-writing medium of choice for distressed youth. The economy and symbolism of poetry lend themselves to a personal creative work that can be completed quickly and satisfyingly, and that can contain honesty, emotional complexity, and resolution for our authors. Poetry also has a natural social context that includes sharing and healing. Here are three benefits of writing poetry after trauma:

- People who write poetry after trauma can be helped to integrate feeling and experience, in a way that happily counteracts the challenging problems of fragmentation and confusion.
- People who write poetry after trauma can learn to see themselves, with pride, as individuals who have had difficult experiences—gaining a perspective beyond feelings of hurt, defectiveness, shame, and a sense of personal responsibility.
- For people who write poetry after trauma, the act of writing and sharing poetry with a mentor provides a safe experience where trust can be established and a positive relationship can be built.

These specific benefits of writing poetry after trauma are contained within the benefits of writing poetry in general, where poetry provides opportunities for being heard, gaining insight, building strengths, and deepening relationships. See the textbox "The Benefits of Writing Poetry."

And So We Begin

Teachers and counselors encounter experiences of terrible hurt in their work with youth (and perhaps in their own lives). It is difficult to know how to respond. Many young people have suffered tragedies that can't be undone. They face a lifetime of effects. Yet, teachers and counselors want to help sufferers adapt and grow in their lives. Helpers want to make things better for the victims, though they may not always know how to deal with the victims' difficulties or with their own feelings in these situations. It is natural for teachers and counselors, as witnesses of others' helplessness and pain, to feel helpless and in pain, as well.

Fortunately, expressive writing is a tool that changes the nature of a terrible hurt, so that the hurt becomes a springboard for emotional growth, pride, and relationship—in a personal evolution that enables new skills and competencies. In this way, through expressive writing, teachers and counselors can serve distressed youth and themselves.

The Benefits of Writing Poetry

- Poetry provides a cultural context and expressive model that supports openness and emotional honesty.
- People who write poetry feel listened to and not judged.
- People who write poetry exercise insight and sensitivity, sometimes in profound and illuminating ways.
- The act of creating poetry reinforces ego strengths, including realizations about who I am, what I think, what my life has been like, what I want, and what I can accomplish.
- Writing poetry is a natural process for people in pain.
- Writing poetry is a natural process for people who are developing an identity and/or seeking understanding.
- Poetry provides a safe and private experience, with individual control over the outcome.
- Poetry provides a basis for greater interpersonal communication about personal issues and for stronger relationships.
- People who write poetry use a variety of cognitive skills.
- In an appropriately structured program, poetry can be used by individuals with severe emotional difficulties and/or poor cognitive skills.
- Writing a poem is a concrete accomplishment.
- A person's purpose in writing a poem can be altruistic, educational, inspirational, etc.
- The accomplishment of a poem can be publicly recognized by saving, sharing, reading, posting, publishing, etc.
- The act of creating poetry is joyful and self-reinforcing, even when the content is about a sad or traumatic event.
- People who write poetry can become more in touch with larger issues of life's meaning and connectedness, developing a spiritual appreciation of life.
- The act of writing a poem is a skill that people can use to help themselves over and over again throughout a lifetime.

2

Pongo, Openness, and a Unique Joy

Strength
by a young woman, age 16

I can be as strong as concrete, a solid brick wall,
  like the ones that I have built to surround me.
Ready to lock myself within the walls, protected, and unhurt.

I can be as strong as the ocean waves,
  that swallow me up whole.
Pay attention to my craving waves, the ones that come after you,
  not giving time to breathe.
I will overcome this fear.

I can be strong in ways you don't expect.
I can be as strong as the stone heart that I carry on my sleeve.
Able to stay strong and stable,
  through all the hurt that is thrown at me.

My strength can be gentle.
I can only be as strong as myself, my weakest link.
Ready to crack under all the pressure.

I can be strong and change the world.
I can.
And I will.

It's a weighty thing to work with young people who have suffered, especially when a teacher or counselor maintains the necessary degree of receptiveness to the young person's hurt. Expressive writing offers a complementary and compensatory set of rewards, in the context of everyone's vulnerability, including an opportunity for openness and dialogue, including a unique and elevating joy. The Pongo Teen Writing Project has felt this weight and valued these rewards.

The History of Pongo

In 1976 I was in graduate school in creative writing in San Francisco when I volunteered in a school for young teens with special needs. At the school I developed a creative writing program in which I worked with the youth individually, evolving collaborative techniques that are at the heart of Pongo today. I first talked to the youth to find out their interests and then suggested personal topics that drew on their fantasies ("Todd's Drive Across Country," "Rodney's Trip to Mars") or personal experience ("A Letter to My Mom," "A Boy I Like"). I took dictation from them, and in the process often improvised a structure, such as a chronology of events or a list of a teen's wishes. An essential part of this technique was that I asked clarifying questions—about things that were imagined, words that were said, and feelings that were experienced: "What do the Martians look like?" "Why do you think your mom was angry?" I offered lots of examples and creative possibilities, as needed. "Were the Martians green, or blue, or red, or some other color?" "How did you feel—maybe you were angry or sad—when your mom stopped talking to you?" These questions were easy for the teens to answer, but brought personally meaningful detail into their writing. It was here that I started to learn about the power of eliciting personal content within an easy-to-use, supportive creative structure.

As soon as the teens and I were done, there was often a special moment, when the teens felt proud, happy, and open. In that moment, there was a sense of accomplishment and closeness that the teens and I shared. This was my reward. In that moment, our relationship was unencumbered by the frustrations and doubts that often burden the work of adults and struggling youth.

I didn't understand the full value of this work at the time, the value for the teens and for me, and I would not come to truly understand its value for many years. However, one turning point in my understanding did come quickly. I hadn't known this, but half of my students were patients at an adolescent psychiatric clinic at Children's Hospital in San Francisco. I learned about the clinic when the teens' therapists sought me out. They told me that the young people in my poetry program were writing about important issues, in particular issues that were hard for them to talk about in therapy.

I was hired by the clinic and became part of a multidisciplinary team that offered the teens intensive, psychoanalytically oriented help. The teens received individual, group, and family therapy, along with activities therapy that now included expressive writing. From the staff in the clinic and from hospital conferences, I had the unique opportunity to learn about the teens' profound vulnerabilities.

In this clinic I also had the opportunity to understand the staff's vulnerabilities, the pressures on myself and others from exposure to the young people's emotional pain—pain that stimulated sensitivity in us, along our own emotional fault lines. The teens' need to feel loved, to feel capable, and to find purpose was part of an essential human sensitivity, that staff as well as youth experienced in our lives.

Of course as a graduate student in creative writing at the time, I was writing my own poetry. I wrote a collection of prose poems in response to the clinic experience, creating a bestiary whose animal subjects struggled with profound feelings of rage, neediness, and depression. My work, education, writing, and personal evolution complemented one another, and I developed insight into issues that begin early in life, are difficult to master, and affect a person's emotional life, self-image, and progress in the world. I gained some insight into the power of writing in this context, as well.

When I left the clinic in 1983, I went on to a career in book publishing, first in special education and then in computer technology, that culminated in a job as a managing editor at Microsoft Press in Seattle. Before I left Microsoft in 1996, I founded Pongo Publishing, now known as the Pongo Teen Writing Project.

The name "Pongo" comes from a character in my poetry at that time, *The Odd Puppet Odyssey*. Pongo is a puppet, like Pinocchio, who wants to feel more human. At the end of a series of complicated and funny adventures, he discovers the need for compassion.

The Pongo Teen Writing Project

The Pongo Teen Writing Project functions as a stand-alone writing program within institutions and their school settings. The majority of the youth Pongo serves have suffered a variety of childhood traumas, often abuse and neglect. One-third of Pongo's writers have written only a little or not at all before Pongo.

Pongo first establishes relationships with the institutions, working closely with administration and staff. The institutions themselves are complicated and sensitive settings, with important and difficult purposes.

Pongo then carefully selects and trains a team of four volunteers (called "mentors") to work at each site under the direction of an experienced Pongo leader. The five-person team visits the institution together one afternoon per week to write with youth. The mentors all work in the same room, and they meet as a group at the beginning and end of each day. The writing projects run for about six months during the school year.

The mentors write their own poetry, as homework, which they bring in and discuss with one another at the beginning of the day. This process enhances their skills and resilience in working with the youth.

To find youth participants, Pongo pulls young people from a classroom or milieu to work with each week. In this process Pongo introduces its intentions in a particular way, by sharing poetry on emotional themes that are important to youth, and by inviting youth to "Write from the heart about who you are as a person." When selecting youth, Pongo doesn't ask, "Who wants to write poetry today?" but rather "Who hasn't written poetry before?"

The mentors usually work with youth one-on-one, and they use techniques that provide support and structure to the process. For example, they might take dictation or use a fill-in-the-blank framework. In addition to the model of individual mentoring, Pongo teams will sometimes use Pongo techniques with small groups or with a whole class.

In the end, the Pongo authors feel safe and supported. They often write about emotionally significant events that are sad, but the young people report that they enjoy and are proud of their writing, and that the process brings them relief from their pain. Institutions report that the youth are more willing to discuss their issues after writing. The writing mentors feel fortunate to experience an emotional and creative experience that helps the youth and also enriches their own lives.

Pongo has ongoing projects at the King County juvenile detention center in Seattle and at Child Study and Treatment Center (the Washington State psychiatric hospital for children) in Tacoma. Pongo teams have also worked at homeless shelters, a foster-care agency, a juvenile rehabilitation facility, and a resource center for lesbian, gay, bisexual, transgender, and questioning youth.

Pongo's primary purpose is to help its authors understand their feelings, build self-esteem, and take better control of their lives.

Pongo's Outcomes

In 2000, the first time I gave a workshop at the Washington State psychiatric hospital for children, I stood before a group of about thirty teens. We were in a multipurpose room lined with bookshelves. The teens sat in rows. They had pencils, paper, and also books to lean on as they wrote. There were about twenty staff from the hospital and school scattered among the youth and at the back of the room. I shared some powerful Pongo teen poetry about difficult experiences. I explained my purposes—that I ask Pongo authors to write from the heart about who they are.

Before we began to write, two teens raised important issues. These were not challenges or disruptions. They were questions on core matters of trust, a significant moment in our work together.

One teen said he was too angry at staff to write that day. I told him that his feelings were an excellent thing to write about. Then a young woman said, "You probably think we're just a bunch of crazy kids." I said that I believe that people who have difficult lives have important things to say. I told them that everyone has the same concerns in life, about being loved, about feeling capable, about finding purpose.

Then the teens wrote. At first I led several structured exercises, but the teens stopped me. They wanted to write on their own. The room was quiet as the youth worked, except that we paused as people finished a piece of writing and read their words aloud, or asked me to read them. The group applauded every piece of writing and then went back to their own work. The writing included stories of trauma and terrible hurt.

One young man wrote the poem "People Who Die in My Life," included here, about pain and the desire to hurt oneself. The boy was thin, thirteen years old, and after he wrote his poem his hair and face looked wet and slick. At the end of our session the young man's foster mom joined the group. She asked if she could see the boy's poem. When she read his words, she burst into tears.

People Who Die in My Life
by a young man in a psychiatric hospital, age 13

People die in my life.
I can't stop it.
It just happens.
It hurts a lot, and I cry cry cry.
But even after they die,
I try to remember the fun, happiness,
and the good times, and talk about it,
so I don't end up in locked-down facilities
and run away and hurt myself
and try to kill myself and
be dead like them.

When I returned to the psychiatric hospital two months later to lead another writing workshop, one of the administrators pulled me aside. She told me that she knew at least three youth who had had breakthroughs in treatment after the initial Pongo workshop, including the author of "People Who Die in My Life." The boy was a therapy client of this woman, and he had never before been able to discuss the experiences alluded to in his poem. He had already been discharged from the hospital.

Experiences like these have a profound effect not only on the young writers but on the adults who want to help them and who witness this heartfelt expression and personal change.

Youth Served and More

In its first seventeen years, Pongo has worked with approximately six thousand youth, about half in one-on-one writing sessions. One-third of our authors have written just "a little" or "none" before Pongo.

Pongo has published five hundred young authors in thirteen books. Nearly fourteen thousand of these books have been given away to youth at our sites, and also to libraries, agencies, judges, and others in the community. Through the new Pongo website, young people from all over the United States and the world have submitted one thousand poems to Pongo.

In its teacher workshops, Pongo has trained hundreds of volunteers, teachers, and counselors in its methods. At local arts festivals, Pongo has displayed and sold teen poetry and talked to over ten thousand people in the community about the poetry and lives of distressed youth.

Pongo's Surveys

Between fall 2005 and spring 2012, Pongo collected surveys from 726 youth in juvenile detention and the state psychiatric hospital. The responses were uniformly positive. This is particularly significant because many Pongo authors have good reason in their lives to feel confused, angry, and mistrustful. The youth not only enjoyed writing (100 percent) and felt better after writing (83 percent), but they wrote about things they normally didn't talk about (73 percent). The full survey results state the following:

- 100 percent enjoyed the writing experience
- 98 percent were proud of their writing
- 73 percent wrote on topics they don't normally talk about
- 86 percent learned about writing
- 75 percent learned about themselves
- 83 percent indicated that writing made them feel better

- 94 percent said they expected to write more in the future
- 92 percent said they expected to write when life is difficult

Some Research on Pongo

In 2001, Pongo collaborated inside a juvenile rehabilitation facility with psychiatrist Ted Rynearson, who had a Soros Foundation grant to study his Restorative Retelling model for traumatic grief therapy (Rynearson 2001). Traumatic grief is the difficult grief a person experiences after a sudden, violent loss, such as a loss from murder or suicide. Over half of the young people in prison have suffered exposure to violent death (Steiner, Garcia, and Matthews 1997).

The study (Rynearson et al., 2006) was not about Pongo specifically, but in three of the four ten-week groups, Pongo writing activities constituted half of the therapy group's time. In all measures of pre- and post-testing, including the Beck Depression Inventory, Inventory of Traumatic Grief, and Revised Impact of Events Scale, the youth in Dr. Rynearson's groups showed a significant decrease in their levels of distress.

In 2006, Miral Luka, PsyD, received Washington State approval to evaluate the work of fifteen Pongo authors at the state psychiatric hospital for children. The youth worked with Pongo during one group session and one individual writing session. Dr. Luka did a textual analysis of the teens' writing and found that the youth not only wrote with depth and detail about their particular issues, but that the creative writing turned out to be a more complete and descriptive representation of a teen's issues than the reported diagnosis.

In her conclusion Dr. Luka (2006) wrote,

> I found Pongo to be a relevant, effective tool for helping youth thoughtfully connect with their past difficult experiences, current mental health issues and salient behavioral issues, and, in a field where establishing rapport and getting teens to open up is an accomplishment worthy of its own glory, to have great capacity to be used as a tool to connect adults and such youth in the midst of their experiences. (page 3)

Current Program Evaluation of Pongo

Today, with help from psychiatrists Dr. Mick Storck and Dr. Liz Koontz of the University of Washington School of Medicine, Pongo is contacting people who had previously written with us in the state psychiatric hospital for children, but have since been discharged. Pongo worked with 237 psychiatrically hospitalized youth in 2000–2001 and 2005–2012.

The research team collects data through a twenty-minute oral survey that asks Pongo's former writers about their current involvement in writing, their opinions about the value of writing, and their feelings about the Pongo experience. The survey includes both open-ended questions and yes/no questions.

For the most part, the young people interviewed worked with Pongo only once or twice, with a mean of 1.89 sessions.

The preliminary results of this program evaluation (which is not a formal study) show that, years later, youth remember Pongo, enjoyed the experience, believe in the value of writing, personally benefited from writing, and are continuing to write. Also, the authors' responses to open-ended survey questions identify specific benefits of Pongo and poetry, including finding a safe environment for self-expression, gaining a tool to regulate emotions, finding shared experience with other teens and mentors, and gaining a sense of pride in their creative accomplishments.

One sixteen-year-old young man told us, "I felt relieved about talking about things through writing that I didn't usually talk about . . . Being in such a horrible place and then having all these joyful people come in to help us, it was kind of like an ambulance coming to a car wreck."

Are There Negative Outcomes?

Caring professionals may wonder if there are negative outcomes in the aftermath of Pongo. Do Pongo's authors feel suddenly exposed, vulnerable, alone, and without resources for coping, after they write about personal trauma with Pongo? Do the teens have reason to regret their writing?

In seventeen years Pongo hasn't heard about such problems from youth or staff. In fact, instead of emotional "backlash," agency counselors report quite different findings.

Jennifer Heger, a counselor for homeless youth at Orion Center, where Pongo worked, wrote, "I do not recall any backlash of emotions. My guess is that it is for two reasons. One, the [work] is done in a therapeutic context with trained facilitators; and two, the author controls the experience. Inherently, they can only write as deep as they are ready for . . . . It's a readiness issue (therapeutically, developmentally, emotionally, cosmically, whatever). They titrate it" (personal communication to author, 2012).

Sashya Clark, a mental health professional at King County juvenile detention center, wrote, "In my time here as a counselor, I have never heard about or observed any negative backlash as it relates to working with Pongo. Young people have often commented on the positive experience of writing and creative expression that you all offer" (personal communication to author, 2012).

Vicki Belluomini headed mental health programs at Echo Glen juvenile rehabilitation center, where Pongo collaborated in the traumatic-grief groups with psychiatrist Ted Rynearson. She wrote, "In the years following the work we did at Echo, the only experience I had with kids who participated was continued growth and forward progress. I never heard one kid that fully participated in the group (or their staff) say there was any negative backlash. The group didn't just stir up feelings and then give them no way to express it. Their writing it all down, and fully experiencing the feelings using this modality, IS the soothing" (personal communication to author, 2012).

In addition, Dr. Mick Storck, a psychiatrist from Child Study and Treatment Center (CSTC, the Washington State psychiatric hospital for children), where Pongo has worked beginning in 2000, offered the following ideas about Pongo's therapeutic value. Storck said the writing became a force that helped the teens define their own treatment hopes and goals. He said he could look at a list of Pongo's 200 authors at CSTC and probably recall the times when, on their own, "30, 40, or 50" youth had brought their writing to him to read, including writing that criticized him or the hospital (personal communication to author, 2012).

Storck also expressed the thought that Pongo enlivens the intersection of a number of treatment methods—dialectical behavioral therapy, trauma-focused cognitive-behavioral therapy, motivational interviewing, and adventure-based therapy—in which the healing goal is to create a safe zone for experiencing and sharing risk. The experience of risk, and the effort to help others move through their risk safely, is part of the healing.

Storck described another dynamic area in the process of personal development and healing, a tension between separation and union. Poetry exists in this dynamic realm of the personal and public. He suggested that another reason why Pongo's writers don't suffer an emotional "backlash" in response to the openness of writing is that poetry is transpersonal. The Pongo authors' writing is shared with their peers, it may be published, and it is always a part of the larger goals of Pongo, which include openness and understanding within the larger community. Storck described the group of Pongo authors with words such as "camaraderie," "group productivity," and "social giving."

Comments by Pongo Writers

At the end of the author surveys, there is an opportunity for youth to make comments. In 726 surveys these comments have all been positive. For example, in the latest set of surveys from juvenile detention, over one-third of the surveyed youth wrote comments. Here are a sample:

- This has been a great time, and I have learned that I have a voice.
- I had a really good time writing, and I have learned more about myself.
- Thank you for this experience. I needed it.
- It was relieving just writing.
- You guys help a lot of kids who don't have any way to explain their feelings.
- It was very nice, helped me get some feelings out.
- I think real writers' poems come from the heart.
- Writing is a lesson a person needs in life.
- I enjoyed it. It created a moment of peace in my heart.
- I had fun, and I feel as if I accomplished something.
- It was great. I think everybody needs to write more.

Using Pongo's Methods in Your Classroom or Agency

Although creating your own poetry program, along the model of Pongo, is one option, it is not necessary to create a stand-alone program to utilize the Pongo philosophy and techniques. Here are some ways that teachers and counselors have utilized the information in this book:

- In a very diverse classroom, a teacher incorporated Pongo writing activities into a two-week poetry unit. The demographic makeup of her school was 24 percent white, 23 percent black, 29 percent Hispanic, 23 percent Asian/

Pacific Islander, 1 percent Native American. In the school, 23 percent of students were English language learners. The Pongo activities helped the teacher overcome her greatest challenge, initially, which was to help the youth get started when they felt daunted or overwhelmed. Over time, the teacher introduced poetry concepts to the teens. By the end, the youth expressed and shared, in their poetry, their innermost fears, experiences, and triumphs. They reviewed each other's work and also created an anthology. Through poetry, the teacher got to know her students, and the students made deep connections with one another. The teacher described the unit as "a total success" (Melissa Struyk, personal communication to author, 2011).

- In an agency that provides mentors to at-risk youth, a volunteer established a weekly poetry group on the Pongo model. The youth reached a milestone quickly, when one young man wrote about his sister's murder by her boyfriend. The writing and discussion opened the door for the kids to write about grief and loss in many aspects of their lives. At the same time the process was therapeutic and empowering. The youth excitedly devoted themselves to poetry (and to periodic readings and publications). The teens were so excited that every week they felt reluctant to leave the evening poetry group; when they did leave they opened up to their mentors on the car rides home. The youth named their writing group "Hearts Out Loud." The writing group brought youth and staff together in a way that changed the agency (Robin Brownstein, personal communication to author, 2009a).

- In a classroom of struggling readers and writers, a teacher used poetry by Pongo teen writers to engage her students in literature. The students were from a low socioeconomic demographic, and several had emotional disabilities. The class had great difficulty with the school district's literacy curriculum, but they became immediately engaged when the teacher introduced poems by Pongo writers (from Pongo's website and books). The class worked eagerly to interpret the Pongo poems about difficult life experiences, and after two months they were able to return to the regular curriculum, with the reward that every Friday the teacher would give them Pongo poems to read and discuss (Sarah Geren-Ziegler, personal communication to author, 2011).

- In individual therapy sessions, a therapist was working with a shy and somewhat socially isolated ten-year-old boy who had severe learning issues. The therapist took dictation from the child to create a poem using a Pongo writing activity. The boy lit up when the poem was read back to him, and two weeks later he entered therapy with a stapled manuscript titled "The Poems of My Life," then proceeded to read ten poignant and sophisticated poems to his therapist. The boy said, "Thank you for showing me about poetry . . . . I try not to think of what to write, I just go to a quiet place like sitting on my bed, and I just write what enters my mind" (Robin Brownstein, personal communication to author, 2009b).

- At a girls' juvenile detention center in a foreign country, an American volunteer, who had never taught writing before, created a poetry program on the Pongo model. The volunteer and I met to discuss the Pongo Method for less than two hours before she left on her overseas assignment. This woman wrote, "It has been amazing hearing their stories, witnessing the way in which they open up about very painful details in their past, and seeing their excitement when they see their typed words." The themes in the girls' writing have included sexual and physical abuse, drug use, criminal behavior, and their being teenage widows from gang violence. The volunteer has launched a blog, published poems, and expanded her program to other detention centers in the country (Maria Hoisington, personal communication to author, 2010).

3

The Special Role of the Writing Mentor

Loveless
by a young man in juvenile detention, age 14

Loveless #2

3 words remain unheard, I love you
emotions stay unstirred, I love you
hopes shatter against white cell walls
before I succumb to sleep, icy tears fall
heart cracks and bleeds, I love you
basic unmet needs, I love you
no trust anymore, yet I'm behind locked doors
oh well, whatever, I love you no more

Loveless I May Be

In here, more of my heart is confined than my body.
People abandon me along my road to redemption.
No one to lean on, my life proceeds without me,
leaving me to catch up using collect calls. I'm

so loveless here—past mistakes reap their price
from me with scythes of regret. Loveless I
may be, but I love being loveless, not loving
myself. I'll be out with the roll of the
dice.

In juvenile detention recently I worked with a small, thin young woman who was filled with anger and sadness. She sat at a table with me in her blue cotton detention outfit and plastic sandals. The girl had been in detention, this time, for thirty days so far. Her parents were drug addicts. Her father had been absent from her life. Her mother was always with a boyfriend and never home. This girl had raised her younger siblings. Now, at fifteen, she had already been an opiate addict for two years, and she had an eighteen-month-old daughter. The girl talked about her need to forgive herself and others, but mostly she talked about the need to get on with her life independently, without anyone else. In detention the girl had just been in a fight and blackened another girl's eye.

That was the content of our first poem. I suggested we work on a second poem, and make it about her emotions. She dictated "The White Walls" in which she actually talked about *not* wanting to feel anything, that if she felt emotions she would be overwhelmed and physically ill from her sadness. After she wrote "The White Walls," she said she felt better, and she was proud of her work.

The White Walls
by a young woman in juvenile detention, age 15

I've been here 30 days
In court today it was the first time I heard my mom's voice
In a year
I don't want to feel my emotions
I don't want to dwell on the past
If I felt my sadness
I would feel physically hurt
My body—tense and weak
Feeling dizzy when I stand up

Around my eyes—blackness
It's all sadness

I feel compelled to do something I don't want to do
I'm trying to forgive myself
And forgive everybody around me
I'm not trying to feel my emotions

I feel plain
Like the white walls I stare at every day

If I keep working toward
Not feeling anything
I can keep working toward
Feeling happy

Like our young author, one of the first challenges facing a writing mentor is to be open to the world of difficult feelings. The composer Philip Glass describes the process of creating music as a process of listening to the music that is all around us. He says that music is like an underground river, always there, something he needs to tune in to in order to compose. My own belief is that the world of Pongo poetry is *not* about tuning in to a river of words, but an underground river of unarticulated emotion that rumbles and roars just beneath the surface of our world. We can feel it through the soles of our feet, when we attend to it, and it shakes us.

Being Open to the World of Emotion

For young people in distress—young people who have suffered a variety of childhood traumas—they are often bound up by their difficult emotions:

- They are confused and have a hard time remembering or understanding what happened to them.

- They often experience strong and unattributed emotional consequences, such as rage or anxiety or numbness, that they may not feel able to control.
- They are preoccupied by and struggling with the circumstances of their emotional lives, as they work to adapt and survive.
- They find that the world is not an accepting place when it comes to their expressions of personal pain.
- They do not have good outlets for their emotions, unless they find a form such as poetry.

To facilitate expressive writing by distressed youth, a writing mentor has to be able to *listen* to what teens need to say in their poetry, even though it includes intense stories of confusion, hurt, and helplessness. A compensating effect is that the teens' openness is a source of relief and joy for them. It becomes a way of relating, healing, and finding purpose.

An adult's ability to listen to difficult emotion is a great gift to the youth, but it is not easy for the mentor. It can make the mentor anxious. She may not know what to do, and she may feel she should do something. It's an unusual thing to hear such heartfelt expression.

The act of listening to someone else's difficult emotion can remind a mentor of her own pain. She may have experiences in her own life, including violence or betrayal or shame or guilt or insecurity, that are evoked by someone else's story. There may be experiences that a mentor has not completely remembered or worked through for herself.

On the other hand, though listening to suffering youth is difficult, it also promises great benefit to the adult writing mentor. Just as lifting a weight builds muscle, holding an emotional weight builds emotional strength. A mentor learns that she cannot always act to change a situation. This lesson can ameliorate some of her anxiety over the need to *do* something. Instead, the mentor is confronted by the philosophical and spiritual challenges of things that are beyond her control. Also, a mentor is opened up to her own experiences and emotions, and helped to grow. A mentor can be personally helped as she helps the teens.

Honoring the world of emotion, for everyone, is a core value of the Pongo Method.

Understanding Our Role as Poetry Facilitators

While writing mentors have to be open to the world of emotion, becoming good listeners, it is also critical that they understand the value and constraints of their role as writing facilitators. Mentors are listening to distressed youth in the context of helping them find their voices, not for purposes of stepping in as advisors, however well-intentioned. *Listening* is the way to do good.

Youth in distress struggle with mixed feelings about their issues, difficulties controlling their behavior, low opinions of themselves, and deep pain in the context of their relationships. These are conditions with deep and complicated causes, without simple solutions. Many times when adults try to help, the youth feel judged. They feel alone and misunderstood. They want to run away.

Here is the difference between the writing mentor's role with a youth and the role of an advisor: The writing mentor does not attempt to offer solutions or redirect the pain. The writing mentor recognizes that he is not a life counselor, nor a problem solver.

Figuratively (and perhaps literally), the writing mentor is sitting next to a youth, and they are working together on the external object of a poem, a piece of paper that sits in front of them. The writing mentor is interested in what the teen wants and needs to say, and makes that expression possible. The mentor supports and appreciates the teen's words, while explaining the opportunity and method of poetry.

In this context, through writing, the teen writers will openly articulate their own experience and difficult emotions in poetry, perhaps for the first time, and thus feel heard. They feel more whole. They feel some mastery over their experience and emotion, they learn about themselves, and they find purpose and direction for their own growth. They discover that the act of writing can be transformative.

Although the mentor's role is to listen, support, and not to advise, an adult mentor does have ethical and legal responsibilities to keep a young person safe. A mentor should report situations where a youth is currently at risk, or where a youth poses a risk to herself or others.

Learning How to Respond to Pain

What does the role of listener feel like and look like? What does a mentor say when a youth expresses strong emotions? What if the teen's emotional state is at or approaching crisis? First of all, it's important to understand that one of the great benefits of poetry, for everyone involved, is that poetry is about feeling. In fact, the feelings that poetry evokes are a measure of its quality. This ability to feel is something that mentors represent to the youth as well as teach, so mentors are allowed and encouraged to have feelings in response to teen poetry. Being a good listener does not mean being cold emotionally.

On the other hand, if a mentor hears a teen's terrible story and is affected, he is called upon to be patient in experiencing his emotion. He needs to be able to sit with his feelings, to share an emotional moment with the youth. Mentors should not talk about themselves with youth, or interrogate the youth about their lives, or judge the other participants in their story (e.g., parents or police). A mentor's anxious reaction might suggest that he is being hurt by the teen's poem, that the poetry experience isn't safe. Rather, mentors want to be present and mostly quiet so that the teens can sense the mentors' natural empathy and feel the healing power of being heard and cared about.

And if a mentor feels the need to say something, what are some things to say? The emotion can be a great context for praising a teen's work. The mentor could say something like "Wow, this poem communicates a lot of feeling. It's very good." If the poem is deeply moving, the mentor could say, "I'm so sorry you had this experience."

These feelings, actions, and responses will fit the great majority of poetic interactions with youth.

Although expressive writing has never evoked a crisis in Pongo's experience, in rare cases a youth comes into the poetry session in a state of emotional crisis. An author in crisis might express suicidal thoughts, profound confusion, and/or ideas that are strange, terrifying, violent, deeply depressed, or paranoid.

Pongo projects are set up to respond to this circumstance. The projects are established to include a mental health contact within an agency, someone who knows the youth. The projects themselves are led by an experienced Pongo facilitator who is a guide and resource to the mentors on the team. The writing sessions with youth begin with some general understanding about safety and confidentiality, including the need to protect those who may be at immediate risk. It is Pongo's experience that youth do understand such safety issues, from their previous experience in the justice and mental health systems.

So how does a writing mentor feel, and how does she respond, when a youth is in crisis? The nature of poetry as a feeling medium, and a mentor's ability to be open to her own feelings in this work, mean that a mentor can use her intuition to help her identify a crisis situation. A mentor can trust her sense of discomfort and concern. If she worries about a youth, the mentor should talk to her colleagues, starting with a project leader who can consult with a mental health professional.

With a youth in crisis, a mentor might ask the youth a few questions to help assess the situation, including, "How do you feel about your poem? Have you ever talked about this with anyone before? Do you have anyone to talk to about this now?" After the writing session, when the mentor talks with others about what is best for the youth, she can also share the youth's poem, as a snapshot of the teen's current emotional state.

Taking Care of Ourselves

There is a challenge in being open to the world of emotion, and there is a challenge in learning the role of poetry facilitator. Ultimately the writing mentor, as listener, is a container for a teen's sometimes difficult feelings. By holding a young person's feelings in this way, the writing mentor validates a teen's voice and constructive self-expression. But there can be sadness for the mentor, along with the rewards of improved engagement and outcomes with youth. Here are some ideas about how mentors can take care of themselves.

Understand your relationship with sadness. Sadness, though painful, does not have to be avoided. It isn't fatal. Rather, it provides a rich experience and an opportunity to deepen one's involvement and sensibility in the world. Mentors can learn to sit with their sad feelings.

Build a community of other mentors. Mentors can also take care of themselves by having a community of other mentors, with whom they share the experiences of this work. At Pongo, our mentors work in teams, and these teams meet at the beginning and end of each day. Pongo establishes projects that include mental health professionals as team members or consultants.

Vary the intensity of the writing opportunities. During the holiday season and periods of great stress for the youth and mentors, Pongo is more likely to introduce lighter or humorous writing themes, consciously responding to the needs of the community. The reality is that many of Pongo's authors have experienced disappointments, including neglect and family turmoil, during special occasions. Pongo has met youth who have never had their birthdays celebrated or received gifts of any kind.

Be mindful of opportunities to praise the positive. A mentor should always stay open to and be aware of opportunities to welcome and articulate sources of resilience for the youth. A mentor almost always has opportunities within the facilitation of a poem to ask the teen about his wishes for the future, to help the teen identify the strengths she showed in a difficult situation, and to assist the teen in imagining the good as well as the bad in a particular condition. The choice of including resilience in writing has an important emotional benefit for the mentor, too.

Have clear end points. Mentors take care of themselves by having beginning and ending dates for their poetry projects. Pongo runs projects weekly for six months, from October to April. A mentor's commitment is for the six-month term of the project only, and later he or she can enlist for the next year. Another way that poetry projects can be run is in ten-week sessions, with breaks in between.

Use personal therapy, if needed. Mentors may need to enter personal therapy, especially if their exposure to the teens' trauma brings up buried trauma of their own.

Write poetry. Finally, mentors can take care of themselves by writing their own poetry, like the teens. At Pongo, each of our teams has a project leader who gives the mentors writing assignments, and the mentors share their own writing with one another as part of their group meeting at the start of the day. In this way, the mentors not only hone their poetry knowledge, but find important opportunities to express how they feel.

What Pongo Looks For in Its Volunteers

Pongo seeks mentors who are capable of their own introspective process, who have learned and are learning about their own vulnerabilities, and who can translate their self-awareness into empathy for others. There is a kind of humility implicit in this level of self-understanding. Also, our mentors must have good boundaries, so that their own needs don't spill over inappropriately into their work with youth. And they must be able to communicate with their peers about the challenges of the work. The Pongo mentors must adapt to complicated environments inside institutions. In addition, Pongo looks for mentors with experience in one or several areas—working with distressed youth, teaching, and counseling. Pongo seeks mentors who have written creatively, especially poetry, and who will write as part of their Pongo commitment. Finally, Pongo looks for volunteers who commit to the project for its term, including being present and on time. This last requirement is not only a practicality for the project, and a support for the other mentors in this difficult work, but it is also a way that Pongo models constancy for our teen authors, who have sometimes never had reliable people in their lives.

4

Poetry as the Expressive Medium

How Tucked in the Corner
by a young man in juvenile detention, age 13

You see that I'm alone
You see that I steal
But you don't know me.

You would know me if
You knew how hard it was to be alone
You knew how love has hurt me
You knew your mom didn't love you.

You see that I smoke
You see that I fight
But you don't know me.

You would know me if
You knew how I turn emotions to haze
You knew how I don't fear death
You knew how tucked in the corner was sadness.

The Pongo Teen Writing Project uses poetry as our expressive medium with distressed youth. There are practical reasons for this choice, but especially, there are therapeutic and creative reasons, where the emotive, subconscious, and symbolic nature of poetry can open the door to revelations of complicated personal truth.

Consider the poem "How Tucked in the Corner," written by a thirteen-year-old boy in juvenile detention, in collaboration with a Pongo mentor. The young man was new to poetry, and he created the piece in a typical Pongo time frame of less than one-half hour. The content and structure of the poem evolved with the help of the mentor, who asked questions and made suggestions, following the Pongo Method. Through this poem the boy was able to explain for himself, and to the world, that he was angry because he felt unloved, and that behind his angry behavior (stealing, smoking, fighting) he was profoundly sad.

The poetry form is uniquely able to facilitate effective, personal, revelatory art. This chapter discusses the inherent value of poetry for distressed youth, including the facts that poetry can

- produce a personally meaningful result quickly;
- use emotional honesty to be easily effective;
- move naturally toward a culminating moment of awareness;
- convey complicated, difficult, and unconscious emotion; and
- provide a healing social context for its emotional openness.

A Poem Can Be Completed Quickly

The fact that a poem can be completed quickly has both practical and therapeutic value. A poem can be completed quickly because of its physical brevity, but more importantly because of its emotional economy, where a lot of meaning is contained in rich poetic techniques and symbols.

In institutions such as juvenile detention or a homeless shelter, the mentor may only have thirty minutes (or less) with a teen in which to facilitate a poem, after which the teen may never be seen again. In detention, the mentor works within the constraints of a system that limits access for reasons of safety and procedure. In a homeless shelter the teens are always free to wander in and out to grab food, check in with friends, or have a cigarette. Fortunately, in a very brief time the Pongo Method can be used to complete a poem—one that is meaningful for the teen, with fresh insight into his life—while simultaneously modeling for the teen a poetic methodology he can use in the future to deal with distress.

But, beyond the practical constraints of time, there are therapeutic reasons why it is useful to work quickly and effectively to help teens describe their important emotions. The teens with whom Pongo works are understandably afraid of failure, but perhaps more than that, they believe that they will fail. They feel defective, and they expect to be criticized, judged, and rejected. Also, these youth are burdened by the feeling that they deserve their pain. The Pongo authors are hurting terribly, in the moment. But when they are helped to succeed quickly, they are both encouraged and soothed, in a way that facilitates their discovery of their own voices and that develops their resilience.

A Poem Is Fueled by Emotional Honesty

It's in our nature as human beings, especially when we're children, to feel responsible for the ways that we are hurt. As a result young people can feel defective and ashamed when they have been abused, as if the abuse is their fault; and in these circumstances young people can experience their own emotions as something wrong in them, as billboards of their failures. They feel condemned by their own hurt, and can shut down emotionally. They can turn inward—feel numb or overwhelmed inside. In this state, young people may not know their own feelings. This is the dilemma of many Pongo authors.

But it is also in our nature as human beings, when in pain, to articulate who we are, to explain our lives and our place in the world, which is a path toward healing and growth. Pongo has seen this tendency toward healing and growth repeated thousands of times with Pongo's authors, when they are given appropriate encouragement and support.

Poetry is an excellent vehicle for expressing oneself in response to pain. Personal poetry is fueled by honest emotion, and it requires very little poetic technique beyond this emotional openness to achieve a good and useful result. This is the core of the Pongo Method, to first facilitate openness, for the sake of a poem, and then to facilitate poetic technique.

A Poem Moves Naturally Toward Awareness

There exists a natural desire in us, when we are hurting, to explain our lives and our place in the world. This explanation is driven by painful emotion, but importantly, it is more than a simple articulation of emotion. Neither is it a simple collection of facts about our lives. The explanation requires an integration of emotion with experience: *What happened in our lives? How did it affect us? And how does it affect us today?*

Ultimately, because this explanation of ourselves is driven by previously unarticulated pain, the explanation itself is at the cutting edge of our understanding. It progresses toward a moment of awareness. When we assemble the pieces of the puzzle that is our life, what do we learn? This is the substance of our story. Discovery is inherent in personal poetry.

Once at juvenile detention I worked with a young man who was very nervous and distractible. When I tried to talk with him, he referred to how complicated his life was, but he could not focus. So I suggested we write a poem about the ways that his life was complicated. I asked him to describe just one way that his life was complicated. I helped him focus and wrote down his words. Then I asked him to focus on another complication. At the end, I asked him to describe a final complication in his life, which turned out to be the time the boy's father threw him through a wall and then walked out of the boy's life. Here is his poem.

Life's Complications
by a young man in juvenile detention, age 13

One complication
Is not having a parent there
Having to live on my own
Having to take care of myself

Another complication
Trying to get over a drug that
Can kill me
And putting my life at risk
Having to go to treatment
And take medication
I wish I never did take
That first hit

A third complication is that
Since I was born
I had to see a lot of abuse
My dad abusing my mom
Abusing me, abusing my sister
A lot of alcohol in the house
Which caused my family
To split up when I was three

Another complication
Is being locked up
Dealing with stress and detention
For getting kicked out of school
They're trying to charge me
For something I didn't do,
Which is "illegal burning and explosives"
It was a friend of my friend
Who lit the garbage can on fire

The biggest complication
The last time I saw my dad
My last picture of him
Is him throwing me through
A sheetrock wall
That's a real complicated picture
And one I'm still trying to get over

Dedicated to my mom

Significantly, this process of going deeper and deeper, of moving toward a moment of particular self-understanding, happens *within* the poem itself. In a good writing process, perhaps encouraged or facilitated, a writer begins with some openness, but moves in the direction of a culminating insight within the poem. The poem's concluding impression on the reader contains its ultimate, and possibly very dramatic, truth. This natural outcome is sometimes surprising for both the writer and the reader.

A Poem Has Complicated and Unconscious Content

A poem can have great meaning, even when it's short. It can be driven by emotional openness, in response to the poet's pain. It moves toward personal awareness, in a dramatic ending. All of these benefits are the product of a poem's ability to contain complicated and unconscious content, which in turn is the product of the rich poetic form.

Consider the meaning implicit in line breaks. When a Pongo mentor is taking dictation, she will record the poet's words in the fragmented lines of a poem, not in complete sentences, and she will use line breaks to reflect pauses and emphasis in the poet's speech. In the poem "Life's Complications" one can see the difference between putting the poet's last thoughts on one line, such as,

That's a real complicated picture, and one I'm still trying to get over

versus putting the last thoughts on two lines, with an implied pause

That's a real complicated picture [PAUSE]
And one I'm still trying to get over

Meaning is captured in a poetic technique such as a line break. Imagine that the last line above ("And one I'm still trying to get over") was spoken softly by the poet, perhaps out of shame or doubt. Suppose it was spoken while looking at the ground. Though spoken softly, the last line may incorporate the poet's significant regret and pain. A pause, in the form of a line break, can represent the poet's complicated and unconscious relationship to the content of his story.

Similarly, there's an effect of rhythm in poetry. Looking at the opening poem "How Tucked in the Corner," there is an increasing intensity between the first two stanzas and their repetition at the end. But even within the poem's structure, the lines that describe other people's perceptions of the poet (beginning "You see that I . . . / But you don't know me") are more passive than the lines that describe the poet's truth ("You would know me if / You knew . . . "). The strength of the poet's own truth, over the perceptions of him by others, is conveyed by the order of the lines, and further emphasized by the repetition. Again, a poetic technique, rhythm, can communicate a poet's very special relationship to the content of his story.

The most dramatic poetic technique, from the perspective of incorporating complicated and unconscious personal content, is the use of poetic imagery, such as simile and metaphor. Take the example of a simile about love, that begins "Love is like . . . ." What does it mean if "Love is like sleeping on a cloud"? What does it mean if "Love is like drowning in an ocean"? What does it mean if "Love is like having a party in a warm, bright house while a storm batters the world outside"? What does it mean if "Love is like being lost and battered by a storm"?

When a Pongo mentor is helping a teen tell his story, and has facilitated emotional openness, it's possible to encourage poetic imagery that reflects difficult personal feelings that have never been consciously articulated before. These feelings may be so knotty and so emotionally challenging that they may be almost impossible to express in any way other than as a poetic image. Imagine a child who both loves a parent and also feels betrayed. Suppose a child senses a parent's emotional disturbance, and feels protective of the parent, but is also filled with anger because the parent was abusive and hurtful. For the child, these conflicting emotions are not only coexistent, but bound together, and intensified by that state of bondage. A poetic image can tell that story, of a deep, unsatisfied, and intensely conflicted need—a need that's like standing in a storm on the rim of a yawning void.

Consider the poem "Lost Memories." The poet was helped to develop similes that describe his dad, his mom, and himself. The similes say important things about the dad's viciousness (scorpion), the mom's elusiveness (snake), and the boy's stubbornness (bull); and significantly, the images combine in the context of the poem to convey the young man's hurt. The young man is isolated by his dad's anger and his mom's abandonment, and he acts thoughtlessly and impulsively himself, in a pained response. No wonder he is lonely and depressed.

Lost Memories
by a young man in juvenile detention, age 17

My dad was like a scorpion
Because he didn't think twice.
It was like I wasn't even there.
He would come home, break things,
Yell, fight, or not come home at all.

My mom was like a snake.
She ran away from problems.
I wondered if she cared because
I never heard from her when she
Disappeared.

And I was fighting out the anger like a bull.
I didn't know what to do
But follow in my Dad's footsteps,
Waiting until I heard from Mom again,
Lost, lonely, depressed.

Line breaks, rhythm, and imagery are examples of three of the poetic techniques that enable complicated and unconscious content in a poem.

A Poem Has a Healing Social Context

When a young poet works with a Pongo mentor, the accomplishment of creating a poem is rewarding, but especially in the context of a validating, shared experience. A person feels vulnerable when she expresses her emotions on intense and painful matters, of course. But when the creative work is shared and respected, a core aspect of the poet's humanity is not only validated but allowed to blossom. In addition, there is a shared social purpose in poetry. The intention is greater than oneself. Poetry *does* change the world, as evidenced by the Pongo mission.

I remember a poetry finale at the state psychiatric hospital for children, when all the youth were gathered to hear each other's poems, as Pongo wrapped up for the school year. One young woman asked her teacher to read her poem to the group, while the girl stood at the front of the room, behind her teacher and between two of her friends who gave her emotional support. Her poem was called "Why I Hate Basketball," and it was about being raped when she was very young and alone with a boy on a basketball court. After the girl's poem was read aloud, and the other teens applauded, the girl smiled sweetly with pride and pleasure. This was a miraculous moment, but one that is repeated over and over, as a core experience of the Pongo Method.

5

The Pongo Approach to Teaching Poetry

There Had to Have Been
by a young woman in juvenile detention, age 14

There's no important person in my life.
There just isn't.
Hasn't always been this way.

At some point there had to have been a person
That made me feel
Happy.
As happy as my splat pink hair.

At some point there had to have been a person
That made me feel
Loved,
As loved as a small baby bluebird
In Mama Bluebird's nest.

At some point there had to have been a person
That made me feel
Important,

As important as The President
At her inauguration.

Right now
There's no important person in my life,
But at some point
There had to have been.

Pongo's volunteers say that the first time they sit down to write with a youth, whether it's in juvenile detention or the state psychiatric hospital or another site, the process feels miraculous.

What makes the Pongo Method so hopeful is that distressed teens have a natural desire to engage in a healing process of self-expression, in which they can explore and explain themselves and their place in the world. They need and want this process deeply, though perhaps not consciously. But the teens need to feel safe, understandably, before they can express themselves openly in this way. In other words, for distressed teens, the writing process can flow naturally, like water flowing downhill, but the teens often need help removing the dams of their confusion, doubt, and fear. The Pongo approach removes these blocks with two essential sets of practices.

First, there is a foundational set of attitudes for the writing mentors, called *Accepting Self-Expression.* A mentor's ability to listen intensely, for example, helps a young person feel respected and appreciated for what she says and feels.

Second, the Pongo approach has an essential set of techniques for writing activities. These techniques are called *Jumpstarting Creative Flow,* and they provide appropriate writing structures, themes, and ideas for the youth. For example, a writing structure might be a fill-in-the-blank poem, which is easy to use; and the theme of that poem might be a feeling that is deeply significant but often unexpressed, such as the feeling of being misunderstood. These techniques help a young person to recall and communicate important experiences and feelings, creatively.

There is also a third aspect of Pongo's approach, called *Honing the Writing Craft,* that is explained briefly. This aspect is often not applicable in short-term work with Pongo's very distressed authors.

The Pongo approach is summarized in figure 5.1, Gold's Triangle.

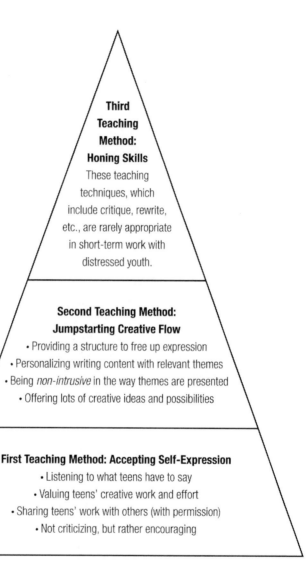

FIGURE 5.1
Gold's Triangle

Accepting Self-Expression

To facilitate expressive writing for teens at risk, it's necessary for a mentor to begin by helping the teens feel that they and their words are respected. Pongo describes these initial attitudes as *Accepting Self-Expression*, and they are foundational. For teens who have been hurt badly as children, and who are confused and self-protective, they need desperately to know that their words are valued. By itself, the experience of feeling respected and being heard can change a person's life.

The simple act of showing an interest in teens' writing, with appreciation and without a critical attitude, can encourage significant personal expression by youth. For example, one of the language arts teachers in juvenile detention once asked me how to teach poetry. I hadn't yet begun training or teaching people the Pongo Method, and I stammered. But what happened later was very interesting: This teacher began saving the poetry that teens brought to him, poems facilitated by Pongo and by other teachers. Whenever a student in his classes finished an assignment early, the teacher would show the student a three-ring binder in which he'd collected other teens' poetry. He would invite this teen to write her own original poetry to add to the binder. With this simple support, teens began writing more and sharing their work. The teacher became a locus of poetry in the school, just because he welcomed, shared, and saved the student writing.

Pongo describes its four foundational qualities of *Accepting Self-Expression* as follows:

- Listening to what teens have to say
- Valuing teens' creative work and effort
- Sharing teens' work with others (with permission)
- Not Criticizing, but rather encouraging

Listening

A mentor's ability to listen is the most important quality for facilitating writing by teens at risk, but it requires careful thought about what listening really means. Many of us share the belief that listening is good, and assume that we're using the skill similarly, when actually we listen with different, unknown constraints on our ability to hear.

When mentors work with teens who've been hurt, they might feel uncomfortable with the sadness that the teens' stories arouse in them. They might feel anxious and want to change the teens' painful situations, which stimulates a desire to assert control and to offer advice. Mentors' discomfort, anxiety, and need to control are natural responses to what distressed teens say, but they are reflections of the mentors' own needs and can interfere with their ability to listen at the deepest level.

In the Pongo context, "listening" means giving serious attention to a young person in a way that includes feeling and empathy, but with a degree of patience. A mentor doesn't need to direct the teen on how to change her behavior. Rather, the mentor helps by bearing witness to the teen's pain as expressed in her poetry. The mentor has to have faith in the value of this process. The mentor's role is explained in chapter 3.

Of course, an adult who listens to a teen's traumatic experiences when they are expressed in a poem ends up with his own important needs, including the need to deal with his own painful feelings and anxiety for the teen. The adult can most appropriately deal with these needs by talking to colleagues, outside the interaction with the teen.

Valuing

With the quality of "valuing," an adult is recognizing the significance of a teen's self-expression, as well as the risk and courage that it takes for a distressed teen to write in a personal way. It's important for an adult to be consciously present, always, when a teen hands him a poem or reads a poem. The young person deserves the mentor's attention, appreciation, and gratitude *at that moment* for sharing her work.

It's also important for a mentor to offer sincere praise when she reads or hears a teen's poem. Perhaps it seems impossible or dissembling to always offer sincere praise. To begin, however, it's a reality that writing itself is hard. It's a reality that writing can be an extremely brave act. These truths can be recognized. In addition, a mentor can almost always find specific aspects of a teen's poem (even if only a single word or image) that are most effective for the mentor as a reader. The mentor can communicate what she particularly likes. And very often, the mentor can identify qualities in a teen's poem that, *by any measure*, are moving, unique, creative, and honest. There is much to praise when distressed teens express themselves bravely and openly.

The ability of an adult to value a teen's work might also require some understanding of the stages it may take to develop trust. In Pongo's experience a teen may begin his creative efforts by offering a poem that is less personal, as a way of testing the poetry waters. For example, one day I observed a teen at the state psychiatric hospital sit down with a Pongo mentor in a one-on-one session and begin his dictation by reading from a dictionary. I understood the need. At the next writing session, when the teen felt safer, he told the story of finding the body of a friend who had committed suicide.

Sharing

Providing opportunities for youth to share their poems is an important validation for them. When teens happily read their work (or allow a mentor to read their work) to the group at the end of a writing session, and are applauded by their peers for their honest self-expression, that is a unique and meaningful reward. The writing group and classroom are wonderful contexts for sharing.

Also, Pongo will type up all of the teens' poems, often during or immediately after a session, and give each teen multiple copies of her work. The teens will proudly share their poems, even personal poems, with family, friends, and helpers. An individual's typed poems will instigate self-esteem, meaningful dialogue, and understanding.

Sometimes the act of sharing is even more basic. In its work Pongo saves all of the teens' poems, which sends a significant message of support to the youth, especially to young writers who may have never had a parent proudly display the child's work on the family refrigerator.

Formal publication is a huge encouragement, of course, and an important component of Pongo's work. But an adult does not have to create books of teen writing, in the way Pongo does, in order to support young writers. There are many other ways that a writing mentor can recognize young authors by sharing their work in the wider world. These ways include organizing a reading, posting work on a bulletin board, publishing a poem in a newsletter, or creating a stapled classroom publication.

It's important to understand that there are many considerations associated with sharing and publication—including the wishes and best interests of the teen authors, the legal requirements to protect teens' confidentiality, and the need to honor teens' copyrights. See chapter 15.

Not Criticizing

Taking into account the profound hurt and deep shame suffered by Pongo's authors, it is rarely appropriate to critique their work. *Any* person, in *any* context, is likely to feel the weight of a criticism, even if it's accompanied by praise. For Pongo's authors, the most important message, and one that will make a tremendous difference to them in their future personal development and academic progress, is that their words have value. Pongo mentors actually fix spelling and make grammar consistent as they type up a teen's poetry. Pongo doesn't want those minor errors to distract from a teen's voice.

Some instructors will understandably feel it's their responsibility to point out errors to help youth learn. Actually, once teens become dedicated writers, there is ample opportunity to teach skills that can make their writing more accomplished. In fact, the best context in which to teach is after the writer is personally motivated. For teens who are at risk, who already feel a crippling amount of shame, *they need to believe in their voices first, before feeling the burden of the skills they lack.*

That said, there are significant ways to suggest changes in a teen's writing and to teach new skills during the writing process. An adult who responds to a teen's poetry from the perspective of *an inquisitive reader, an appreciator*, and *a poetry expert* can impart a great deal of information about poetry without shame for the writer. For example, it's possible for an adult mentor to explain to a teen that, as a reader, he is curious about how the teen felt in the circumstances she describes. The mentor can invite the youth to say more about her feelings, as a way of improving her poem.

As an appreciator of a poem, a mentor can ask for more details and for more examples of experiences to include in a poem. Of course, as an appreciator, a mentor can (and should) ask for more poems, too.

And as a poetry expert, a mentor can illustrate how a figure of speech or a repeated line can add subtlety and emotional weight to a poem.

But all suggestions are offered as an option, as a resource for the poet, not in criticism of what the poet has done. The mentor is always speaking with praise and in support of the poem. And the decision of whether or not to make any changes always rests with the poet herself.

In his role as mentor, the adult is *never* pointing out "mistakes" in order to make a poem better, he is pointing out things he likes, while sometimes offering suggestions that a writer might use, on the writer's own terms. The mentor is always expressing a wish for more writing from the youth.

Jumpstarting Creative Flow

The *Jumpstarting Creative Flow* methods form a guide to creating effective writing activities for distressed youth. The activities will use writing structures (such as fill-in-the-blank poems), relevant themes, and lots of creative ideas, as needed, to give distressed teens a leg up on personal self-expression.

Someone might wonder if these structures, themes, and ideas that Pongo offers are constrictive, an imposition on a young person's self-expression. They are not. Quite the opposite. They are a liberating opportunity. Imagine the difference between asking a child to play in a barren room, and asking that child to play beside you in a sandbox filled with toys. Imagine that the child has been hurt in ways that limit her happy experiences and imagination. The adult companionship and the stimulating environment are kindly, supportive, and encouraging.

Generally, the process of writing does not begin in the vacuum of a blank piece of paper, anyway. Though writing might be created by one person, and though that person might be driven by very private explorations, the writing process is actually informed by a number of worldly influences, including the inspiring models that have come before, the vital interplay of words and ideas among people, and the expected social context for the outcome. The Pongo methods provide models, words, ideas, and many possibilities at the creative moment of a distressed teen's awakening.

For Pongo, there are the four aspects of *Jumpstarting Creative Flow*:

- Providing a writing structure to free up self-expression
- Personalizing writing content with relevant themes
- Being nonintrusive in the way we present themes and options
- Offering lots of creative ideas and possibilities

Providing a Writing Structure

When I worked in an adolescent psychiatric clinic in the late 1970s as an expressive therapist, we took the teens on a camping trip every summer. Many of the teens had never been outside the city before. Many were already affected by deeply troubling and mysterious fears in their daily lives, without the added stimulation of being in a dark woods at night for the first time. To help the teens articulate and manage their fears, I created a ghost story with them that we wrote in the weeks before the trip, with the expectation that we'd read the story aloud at the campfire.

I wrote the architecture of the story, in which the youth went on a trip together into the woods, but I asked the teens to write discrete sections in which they described scary sounds, monsters, and their ultimate conquest in the situation. This ghost story was a writing structure, a clear and evocative form with specific opportunities for writing, through which the teens could easily and enjoyably express themselves. In this natural and flowing context, the teens could include personal feelings and ideas in their responses. They could have fun while imagining ways of defeating the symbolic monsters that terrified them.

Another advantage of a writing structure is that teens can write according to their ability. In the ghost story example, when I asked the teens to complete the sentence "As darkness fell, the campers heard scary sounds like _____," one young man, who had developmental disabilities, dictated one word, "Boo," and one young woman, who was college capable, wrote a descriptive paragraph with owls hooting, trees swaying, and mysterious cracks and rumbles in the forest.

The facilitated creative process can be very surprising, too, as youth open up and are enlivened. One young man, who was always dressed in black and was notably alienated within the community, suggested we have background music for the play. He brought in his favorite heavy-metal music cassettes to share. Each cassette was individually protected in a plastic envelope, and he unwrapped them carefully to play his favorite songs. We listened to his music and chose a selection to introduce our play. The young man's process of sharing, and exposing his musical passion, represented a new relationship between the young man, the group, and the agency.

One young woman, who was electively mute and who had never spoken in front of the group, wrote a part for herself in the ghost story. On the camping trip, when everyone was gathered around the campfire, with a fire blazing and a deep darkness surrounding us, this girl softly read her part. For most of us, it was the first time we heard her voice, and it gave us chills.

Obviously many forms and genres, like a ghost story or play, can provide the forms for writing structures. Pongo concentrates on poetry, however, because a poem can quickly and surprisingly include content that is personal, complicated, and unconscious.

Consider the opportunity provided by a Pongo fill-in-the-blank poem on the theme of "Ten Reasons to Love Me." In this writing activity, created by Pongo leader Ann Teplick, there are lines such as

I may not be perfect, but I can _____

I want the people around me to understand _____

I have unusual ideas, like _____

I have a secret talent, I can _____

This process of completing fill-in-the-blanks makes it easier for a teen to acknowledge her own positive qualities and intentions. Consider how special this positive view of herself might be for a teen, especially if she normally struggles with feeling unlovable because she was once abused. The "Ten Reasons to Love Me" poem can be a revelation to the teen writer about herself, and a revelation to the people who know her.

Of course, the same process works to facilitate sadder feelings that are similarly difficult to access. It is their unacknowledged, sad feelings that are often at the emotional core for teens at risk, and thus at the core of Pongo's mission. The fill-in-the-blank example below is on the theme of feeling misunderstood. It was based on the teen poem "How Tucked in the Corner" that began chapter 4. The structure of the exercise, including the poetic repetition and rhythm, sets an emotional tone for the teen and makes open communication easier.

YOU DON'T KNOW ME

You see that I _____ *(fight, ???)*

You see that I _____ *(do what people want, ???)*

But you don't know me

You would know me if . . .

You knew how hard it was to _____ (hold in my anger, ???)

You knew how I feel sometimes that _____ (no one cares, ???)

You knew how _____ (my dad walked out on me, ???)

You see that I _____ (swear, ???)

You see that I _____ (smoke, ???)

But you don't know me

You would know me if . . .

You knew how I _____ (express myself through art, ???)

You knew how I _____ (like to cook, ???)

You knew how I _____ (take care of my younger sisters, ???)

It's a remarkable aspect of the fill-in-the-blank that many different teens can use the same exercise to write powerful and *individual* poems about their important personal issues. For example, once a teacher had his class send me fifteen "You Don't Know Me" poems. One girl wrote that "you see that I smile" but "you would know me if you knew how my father helped to raise a child that wasn't his but left my sisters and I for four years." One boy shared that "you see how I can play basketball and want to go to college" but "you would know me if you knew how hard it was to be me every day." And another girl wrote that "you see that I always do the opposite of what I am taught" but "you would know me if you knew how my father's death has ruined me."

The fill-in-the-blank method is a clear instance of a poetic writing structure, but there are other structures that Pongo offers its writers. Another technique that Pongo uses, one that is specific to our one-on-one sessions, is that the mentors take dictation from our authors. With a pad and pen in hand (or a laptop), the Pongo mentor will sit with a teen. The Pongo mentor will ask the teen if there's anything on her mind, and when she speaks he'll begin immediately to write down what she says, and evolve it into a poem, using line breaks and selective editing. The mentor will ask clarifying questions and offer suggestions. The process is more complicated than this, of course, but the point is that the mentor's involvement has the potential to make the teen's self-expression both easily conversational and, ultimately, personal.

For example, the mentor will interact collaboratively, as necessary, to ask for elaboration on important points, about how the teen felt in a situation, and what happened next. The mentor's involvement also has the potential to make the outcome more poetic and more complete. For example, in addition to line breaks and selective editing, the mentor will ask for sensory details, etc., that make the writing more effective. In this collaborative context, the Pongo mentor will also teach a teen about poetic imagery, repetition, and other expressive poetic techniques. Such a process is unencumbered and gratifying for a teen.

Writing structures make it possible for distressed teens to express themselves easily and personally. They are particularly successful at facilitating self-expression, in a brief time, that is deep, complicated, and revelatory. Again, the Pongo structures are enhanced, or even made possible, by the methods of *Accepting Self-Expression,* in which the adult mentor listens without judgment, while offering praise and providing opportunities for sharing.

Personalizing Writing Content

The teens with whom Pongo works have suffered experiences like watching Mom being beaten regularly by her boyfriend, or seeing a cousin murdered on the streets, or having an alcoholic father beat them and walk out forever, or being raped repeatedly at ten years old, or having parents who go out at night to feed their addiction without feeding their children. Imagine what it must be like for these young people to sit in school, or in any similarly "irrelevant" context, when they are overwhelmed with worry and pain. Imagine what it must be like for these young people to be keeping secrets, to feel judged for their lack of academic focus or their behavioral challenges, when their deepest need is to understand and address their trauma. In the teens' minds and hearts, what can compete for their attention when they are experiencing terror on the streets or at home?

Teens who are in distress need the opportunity to write about *themselves*, their important issues. This is what is meant by "personalizing the writing content." Nothing is as immediate and necessary. (Importantly, these writing opportunities need to be artfully designed so that they are personally relevant but nonintrusive.) The fill-in-the-blank activities on the Pongo website include poems called "Addicted," "Where I Come From," "Lessons of Courage and Fear," "Inside Me," "When Death Comes Suddenly," "Walk One Mile in My Shoes," and "This Is Who You Are to Me." The themes in these activities are personal, serious, and reflective.

It's important that the teens' writing is reflective. It's personal, but it's about more than themselves, which is an important quality that adult mentors can appreciate and learn from. Adult mentors need to understand that the teens' writing is psychologically, philosophically, and spiritually profound. How do people even begin to talk about terrible events? How can they explain why such things happen? How do they understand their own intensely mixed feelings? What are their deepest wishes and regrets? What are their unacknowledged strengths? How do they imagine a possible future? How do they find meaning in their lives? Adult mentors are challenged to not only recognize and support the young people's deep questioning, that is part of the personal content that needs to be expressed, the adults are challenged to grow psychologically, philosophically, and spiritually along with the youth.

Being Nonintrusive

One of the most important parts of Pongo is that, while the mentors create an opportunity for deep personal expression, they are also purposefully nonintrusive in the process. The Pongo mentors understand that the teens need paths to resilience through expressive writing, *but the teens do not need compulsory (and traumatic) recreations of a trauma.* There is an important distinction here, between allowing teens to express what they need to express and, on the other hand, confronting them with the terror that enshrouds their hearts and minds.

How does one encourage writing about abuse and neglect without behaving intrusively? It occurs in several ways. First, while mentors accept and value personal expression, and while they are ready to bear witness to stories of trauma, the mentors do not require or pressure young people to write about their hurt. For example, mentors never say "You must" write about something painful, and they never say "It would be good for you" to write about something painful. The mentors do say "Write from the heart about who you are," and they invite youth to write about "What's on your mind." While mentors do give the youth models of personal expression, including models of personal expression after trauma, they also *respect the teens' decisions about how and what to write.* The teens will sometimes write about pets, silly moments, and favorite foods. These things are important. Pongo mentors understand that their patience, openness, and understanding, and the sense of safety those qualities can provide, are what make personal expressive writing possible.

Second, Pongo mentors recognize that there can be an evolution to writing openly, and that a teen might begin by expressing something that seems superficial. For example, teens in juvenile detention often begin a dictation exercise by expressing a wish to get out, or by expressing their feelings of boredom. The Pongo mentor will always begin a poem where the teen begins her thoughts. As it turns out, using the Pongo Method, a modest beginning will often lead to expressive writing on important topics, sometimes in the same poem. For example, a teen who writes about her frustration with detention can also bring up mixed feelings about the world outside detention; and a teen who writes about her boredom can also bring up emotional numbness, and the fearful experiences that she'd rather not think about.

Third, even when Pongo mentors personalize the content of a writing activity, and create a writing topic that addresses young people's emotional preoccupations, they do not *directly* confront a young person's particular trauma or the betrayal it might contain. For example, if mentors were providing an opportunity for teens to write about mothers, they would never ask youth to "Write about the worst thing your mother ever did." Rather, the mentors might suggest that the teens write down some generalities about mothers, such as what mothers care about and what they don't. The generalities that youth write in this context are often personally significant, such as when a young woman writes that mothers can sometimes care more about alcohol than their children.

There are more ways of being nonintrusive when encouraging self-expression. For example, Pongo's fill-in-the-blank activities will often provide opportunities to write about *both the good and the bad* in regard to a person or situation, the positive feelings as well as the negative. Given this opportunity, teens who are deeply conflicted emotionally will be more comfortable, and expressive. A teen might write that her father is a good person in many ways, though irresponsibly addicted. Sometimes it's simply impossible to make a single-minded judgment about a confusing situation.

Offering Lots of Creative Ideas

Pongo mentors offer lots of creative ideas to initiate and support a writing process. This is important because the nature of creativity is actually very different from the way some people might imagine the process. Some people expect creators to work in isolation in order to achieve great things. Some people think creators should work without others' influence, except when they're in training. Some people worry that the influence of others on a creator might be a form of cheating, might lower the measure of an individual's ability.

Actually, creativity is often highly stimulated by others. Creativity is often a riff on many influences in a creator's life. If there is a powerful flow of ideas in the creator's environment, it can have a constructive effect on the artist's individual creativity.

Pongo mentors never hesitate to provide examples of images, sensory details, and themes, especially if a writer seems to be at a loss. Only a small percentage of the time will the writer select one of these suggestions literally. Most often, the mentors' suggestions stimulate a writer's own creative process. If a mentor models a simile by asking, "Is your anger like a forest fire? Is it like a volcano?" a teen might speak up and say, "No, my anger is like a snake that turns around and bites me."

Honing Writing Skills

The first and most important purpose of the Pongo Method is to help distressed teens feel sufficiently safe and supported to express themselves—to help them describe openly what their lives have been like and how they feel. When teens discover their voices in this way, they are also better able to understand themselves, feel relief, articulate aspirations, and reach out to other people. The teens' discovery of their own voices is transformative.

Looking at figure 5.1, "Gold's Triangle," the first purpose is achieved through techniques of *Accepting Self-Expression* and then *Jumpstarting Creative Flow*. At this early stage of a Pongo writer's development, the role of the writing mentor is to be interested and supportive of writing, uncritically.

Pongo rarely functions outside this early stage. Pongo mentors work in settings such as juvenile detention where there is a rapid turnover of youth. The mentors work with youth who are so deeply hurt that, to begin, they are understandably confused, mistrusting, and inarticulate. Pongo has set the goal of exposing as many youth at our sites as possible to the potential of writing, especially new writers.

Some teachers and counselors, especially if they have ongoing groups, may wonder how to use the Pongo Method to teach writing skills at a higher level. This higher level embodies the techniques of *Honing the Writing Craft*, which build on the foundation of *Accepting Self-Expression* and *Jumpstarting Creative Flow*.

Once teens are motivated and self-confident writers, a teacher or counselor can help them to further hone their craft by providing more models for poem writing, more discussion and drills on technique, more evaluations of an individual's poems by her peers, more opportunities to rewrite, and more opportunities to share. The teens, as motivated writers, can often take the lead in asking for what they need. The foundation for this process always remains the mentor's unflagging interest and support.

6

A Model Pongo Writing Project

Monkey
by a young man in juvenile detention, age 12

When Mom's not home, we go to the park
and pick the plums from the trees.
You like the small ones, but I say
they're not quite ready yet, they're sour,
but you say you like it, you like the sour ones.

The plums aren't there anymore,
all of them fell three weeks before I came here.
We went back to the park, and the plums
were all fallen, all rotten.

It will be summer the next time
we go to get plums from the park.
You'll be six and want to climb the trees
to get them—You also like
bananas, so I call you Monkey.

I miss you.

Dedicated to my sister

The Pongo Method includes the purposes, approach, and specific techniques for facilitating expressive writing with distressed youth. These aspects of the work can be adapted to many classroom and counseling settings, but they are most easily understood in the context of how Pongo operates and Pongo's project structure, including the ways that the Pongo mentors will work with institutions, access youth, organize their time with youth, keep youth safe, and acknowledge the youth writing. The Pongo structure is elaborated here, as a "model" Pongo project.

Many readers will use this project structure literally, as the foundation for their own writing projects on the Pongo model. Many readers, including many teachers and counselors, will generalize from Pongo's use of communication, organization, and management to inform their own use of the Pongo Method in their schools and agencies. For example, teachers and counselors may consider Pongo's structure in deciding how they ally themselves with colleagues in a new writing project, how they set priorities in a writing session with youth, and how they eventually save and share student work.

A Model Pongo Project

Here is the design of a model Pongo Teen Writing Project for distressed youth.

1. A Pongo project leader meets with administrators and staff at an institution or agency, in order to initiate a weekly Pongo project. The Pongo project requires support within the agency and appropriate access to youth. For its part, the Pongo project must adapt to the concerns and purposes of the agency, follow agency rules, and be a good communicator with the agency throughout. It is Pongo's policy to leave copies of teen writing each week in a binder to which agency staff (only) have access.

2. At every site Pongo establishes a relationship with a mental health professional (psychiatrist, counselor, social worker, caseworker, etc.) as an available contact, someone with whom the Pongo mentors can always discuss any questions or concerns about the well-being of teen writers. Safety is discussed in chapter 7.

3. The Pongo leader finds two to four volunteer writing mentors to form a team. The mentors must agree up-front to Pongo's expectations. The team trains in the Pongo approach (chapters 1–5), Pongo techniques (chapters 8–14), poetry skills, and the culture and rules of the host agency. Pongo looks for mentors who are mature, self-aware, sensitive to youth, and creative. Pongo offers about six hours of required training in one or two sessions before its projects start. There is ongoing training in weekly meetings (#18 below). And yes, a person can do a Pongo project at a site by herself.

4. A Pongo team of five will work with five youth each session, so that there is a one-to-one ratio of adults to youth. To find writers, Pongo will often work with teachers in an institutional school, timing its projects during school hours, then pulling youth from class to write poetry. In different contexts, the process of finding young writers may be different. Sometimes youth are encouraged to participate each day from within a milieu such as a drop-in center for homeless teens; sometimes youth are brought to the writing group by their counselors; and sometimes youth have signed up for the writing activity while inside a residential setting.

5. Pongo often works with different youth each week. This is the result of practicalities, such as the high turnover of youth in detention. It is also the result of Pongo's important goal *to teach the process of writing to as many youth as possible*. A program designed in this way, in which the Pongo team works with different youth each week, can create very special opportunities to work with brand new writers who are shy. Youth can be encouraged to try out writing without commitment, yet to great effect.

6. *On the other hand*, a Pongo project can also be established to work with the same group of dedicated writers each week. In one mentoring organization, the same teens wrote together for years, and used the experience to more deeply process their personal trauma. The organization observed that the highly vulnerable young writers were transitioning out of self-destructive patterns and behaviors, and forging new pathways for themselves. Ongoing poetry groups can be used in schools in place of other "social skills" groups that serve youth who require special programming for behavioral issues.

7. To encourage youth to participate in any group, it is necessary to begin with a statement of Pongo values and poetic opportunities that stress a

profound interest in teens' voices. Pongo wants youth to "Write from the heart about who you are as a person." These values, and the words that express them, are explained in chapter 8. This introduction of poetic values might be made to a classroom each week, before youth are pulled to join writing groups. It may be stated at the beginning of the writing group each week, when new or returning youth writers are assembled.

8. To describe Pongo's priorities within a weekly session, the top priority is to have youth write personal poetry one-on-one with an adult, as described in chapters 9–12. The second priority is to have the youth share their writing with the entire group of youth and adults at the end of the session. The third priority is to provide a group warm-up activity at the beginning, before the youth meet individually with the adults. Group writing is described in chapters 13–14. (See #9, below, for fuller depictions of session structure.)

9. As a time requirement, the Pongo session would require from 50–90 minutes, broken down as follows: (1) introduction to poetry (and group culture) (5–10 minutes); (2) group warm-up writing activity (15–20 minutes); (3) one-on-one work of adult and youth (30–45 minutes); (4) sharing of poetry at end of session (10–20 minutes). The time requirements are such that a 50-minute group would focus on one-on-one work and the final sharing. A 90-minute group would include a group writing warm-up, along with more time for one-on-one writing and sharing. See chapter 13.

10. In terms of the physical layout of the writing classroom, the adult-youth pairs need enough space to spread out around the room in relative privacy. Ideally, they have small desks or tables at which they can write together on pads or laptops. (The mentor is always the one who uses a computer, to help the teen focus on her words, not formatting.) Ideally, the group has a large table, or the ability to circle chairs, so that everyone can sit together at the beginning and end of the session.

11. Pongo makes a tremendous effort to provide youth with copies of their writing the same day, or as soon as possible after the writing session. Often the mentors will arrange to type and print the teens' poems at the project site. They then provide the youth with *three copies* of their written work immediately, so the youth have copies to share with friends, family, and counselors.

12. Pongo negotiates with each site about the use of equipment, such as computers and printers. Some sites have a computer room that Pongo can use. Some sites allow Pongo mentors to bring in their own laptops and a Pongo portable printer. Files are saved to Pongo flash drives, not to institutional computers.

13. The mentors save each youth poem using a consistent file-naming convention, by the author's first name. The filename includes the author's first name, the first three letters of her last name, the date, a number, and the initials of the mentor who worked with her. The Pongo project leader will take the flash drives home, save the files to a directory on her home computer, and send the files to Pongo every week.

14. When they type the youth writing, the Pongo mentors are artful: They preserve the teens' idiomatic voices, but fix spelling and grammar as necessary so that irrelevant errors are not a distraction from the poem's content. Editing a teen's poem requires a very light touch. It is not the mentor's responsibility to change the poem into something the mentor might have written on her own. If a poem is published later, the teen's real name is removed to protect her confidentiality. Identifying details are also changed, such as the name of a pet, names of siblings, city of origin, etc.

15. During a Pongo project all teen writing is also carefully and systematically saved in hard copy, with the printed and signed Pongo Writer Release form that gives Pongo permission to publish. A separate form is signed every time a youth works with Pongo and stapled to the author's poems from that day. See chapter 15.

16. A huge encouragement to youth in their writing is to have an opportunity for sharing in the form of a final reading or publication, or both, at the end of a project. This sharing does not need to be expensive or complicated in order to be an effective support. (Sharing might take the form of a posting on a bulletin board.) A final reading inside an agency can include snacks, guests, and readings by agency staff. A formal publication is more challenging because of its public nature and because of the effort and expense required. A publication also calls for particularly close collaboration between a Pongo project and an agency.

17. With publication there are important issues to consider, including permissions, copyrights, and confidentiality. It's good to have any culminating experience in mind, and established as a goal, from the beginning of

a project, in order to prepare as the project progresses, for example by obtaining permissions. It is also important that the writing mentors not over-promise what they can offer the youth. Issues of publication are discussed in chapter 15.

18. In running a project, the Pongo team commits time to meeting before and after each weekly session with youth. In the meeting beforehand (45 minutes) the Pongo mentors share their own poetry, which is written based on an assignment from the project leader; and they also talk about the youth and about poetry skills in general. The advantage of having Pongo mentors write poetry is that it hones their poetry skills for collaborating with youth, and at the same time allows them to process the painful stories they may hear from the youth. In the meeting after the youth leave (15 minutes) the Pongo mentors discuss the day's process, share emotional experiences, and identify any youth about whom they are concerned. The leader can then talk to staff in the institution or agency when the Pongo team feels a youth might need additional support. (*Note: Pongo believes that it is very valuable for adult mentors to write themselves, but it is not an absolute requirement for a successful Pongo project.*)

19. For project length, Pongo's projects generally run for about six months of weekly sessions, from October through April (not including time off on school holidays). By starting in October the project gives a school the chance to settle in at the beginning of the school year. By ending in April, the project can conclude with a final assembly during National Poetry Month. But projects on the Pongo model are often organized in eight- or ten-week sessions, with breaks in between.

7

Keeping Everyone Safe

I Like the Rain More Than the Sun
by a young man in juvenile detention, age 13

Wish my wrist was bleeding
To stop my heart from beating
With a blade or a knife
To end this life
Just being in here
And what happens outside of this place
My dad is a druggie
My mom is depressed
And she hasn't stopped crying
Since I've been here
It's a high chance I'll be found guilty
Like my uncle did when he wasn't guilty
The sad thing is
I've felt this way since I was eight
My cousin abused me every day
And my dad can't do anything
He needs drugs to feel happy every day
I like that it's raining

I like the rain more than sun
I like the rain because I can walk in peace
No one will really bother me
Because no one likes the rain
And because of that I feel no more pain

I remember when I tried to phone a former Pongo writer, for purposes of current research, to find out how his writing was going. I'd worked with him seven years earlier, in the state psychiatric hospital when he was thirteen. I ended up having a long conversation with the young man's mom about his suicide at eighteen.

I remember many such affecting events and interactions over the years. I remember every time a young girl in detention has written about being prostituted by her mother for drugs. I remember when one of my first Pongo volunteers quit on the first day, after explaining that her parents were Holocaust survivors and that the detention environment brought up too much pain to bear.

I remember when I helped a Pongo writer, formerly in detention, to win an award from the mayor of Seattle. Then, when I offered to drive the young man home late at night after the award ceremony, I found myself not at his home but at a seedy motel, where people peered at me from behind torn and yellow window shades, at a location known for prostitution, drugs, and trouble.

I remember that a Pongo volunteer in detention was escorting some youth to poetry, when another youth ran out of a classroom and attacked one of the teen poets. A woman on the detention staff, who tried to break up the fight, was bloodied and ended up with a concussion and two hairline fractures in her back.

After seventeen years of Pongo, the greatest stress I feel is the responsibility for the welfare of terribly vulnerable youth, and for the adult mentors who do this work, for everyone connected to Pongo at agencies and institutions, and for my own reputation as a caring and capable person.

I have always felt risk and responsibility, particularly in the initial years of Pongo, when the teens first wrote openly about trauma. I knew when I developed the Pongo Method that the teens wrote happily and personally, and that the teens and I enjoyed a rewarding closeness in the process. But with my education in English and poetry, not psychology, how could I know that this process of writing about trauma was having a good effect? It was only through the constant support of respected mental health professionals that I could understand Pongo poetry's remarkable and enduring value for the youth, an understanding that is now validated by a long history, research, and a large community of supporters.

Beyond that, the distressed youth themselves and the institutions in which I worked were all mysteries to me at first. Even now, while I know that many youth will eventually grow out of their worst struggles, and that *all* youth appreciate the opportunities of poetry, I also understand that there are many unknowns about any one teen's social adjustment and emotional health.

Also, along the way, at each stage in the development of Pongo, I had to think long and carefully, and seek advice, about what was right and safe to do. These stages included publishing books, taking on volunteers, having a website, inviting poetry from unknown youth on the website, training strangers in the Pongo Method, and supporting projects on the Pongo model.

Safety is a complicated issue, whose range includes legal requirements, restricted environments, emotional vulnerability, impacts on different individuals in different roles, group dynamics, and public forums.

Understanding Laws and Institutional Rules

States have laws that require background checks for volunteers, protect the confidentiality of minors in the juvenile justice and social service systems, describe appropriate behavior for any adult with minors, and mandate reporting of certain risk or abuse. Any adult who works with youth must be familiar with these laws before beginning a teen writing project. It is likely that any agency in which a writing project is placed would provide orientation to these laws, as part of its own policy.

To summarize Pongo's experience, an adult volunteer must be a safe person who will protect a minor's privacy and will not reveal the minor's identity outside the social service facility. There can be no personal relationship between a volunteer and a youth beyond the context of Pongo's work. The adult mentor also has a special responsibility to consider the teens' safety, and to report (rare) situations of immediate risk, such as a young person's suicidal thoughts or current abuse, to people within the institution.

In addition to laws, there are institutional rules that respond to safety, determining when people access the youth, how they move youth, and who needs to know about what is occurring in the moment. At Pongo's juvenile detention project, for example, there are times of the day when the youth are locked in their rooms and unavailable, such as during staff shift changes. There are occasional lockdowns after violent incidents.

Because of changing populations in detention, Pongo doesn't know each week where it will find space to write with youth. The Pongo leader determines a writing location in conversation every session with a detention supervisor. Then the leader goes to the detention school to find young writers. Before moving the young people to a writing location, the leader will check in with the detention staff person who is responsible for the youth, to make sure that the staff person agrees to the move, that he is notified of where the youth will be, and that he can provide input about whether the youth in the Pongo group can be safe with one another. The institution requires that youth walk between locations in single file with their hands behind their backs. Pongo necessarily follows all rules.

Issues of Youth Safety

My first concern for youth safety was the impact on them of discussing personal trauma in their poetry. But Pongo's long history has shown that when mentors follow the Pongo Method, such self-expression is safe. In the Pongo Method, the mentors have roles as facilitators of poetry, not as therapists or advisors. The mentors clarify for the youth the ability of poetry to deal with personal and complicated issues, but they do not pressure youth to write on painful subjects. Given this focus and freedom, the youth write on issues they want to discuss, some of them very painful, but at a level they can tolerate and in a context where they feel proud of what they say.

As it turns out, the more immediate concern for safety of the youth is their mental condition at the moment they enter a writing group. Over a six-month project at juvenile detention, for example, where mentors work with two hundred youth, there are two or three times a year when a youth will write in a way that raises anxiety in a writing mentor that the youth is having a mental breakdown, perhaps is suicidal. The writing does not cause this breakdown.

Another issue of concern is that a youth might write about a current abusive situation. Such writing about current physical risk is rare, possibly because youth understand that it may be reported. But Pongo wants the mentors to respond to their worries for the teens' welfare, as responsible adults.

For circumstances of immediate mental health risk and immediate physical risk, Pongo has reporting policies that vary depending on the setting, as explained below. To begin, however, at every project site Pongo requires that there is a contact on the institutional staff who is a mental health professional and who is available to the mentors to discuss their concerns. Pongo also has mental health professionals on its advisory board.

In terms of the reporting policies for different sites, at the psychiatric hospital, where discussion of everyone's emotional state and safety is an essential part of the culture, Pongo likes to have a staff person on our poetry team who can help select youth participants, evaluate youth, and report issues appropriately. Again, the need to report is rare.

For reporting at the detention center, Pongo's current policy is that at the beginning of each individual writing session the writing mentors will show the youth a blue card that says:

> Dear Writer: We want you to know that this group is a safe place to write about anything, even the most difficult experiences. We will protect your confidentiality on the outside. But we also want you to know that if we worry that you or someone you know is in an immediate life-threatening situation (for example, that someone might hurt themselves or be hurt), we will want to talk to you about it and act responsibly. This does not come up very often. —Pongo Teen Writing

If writing mentors have worries about a youth during the session, they discuss their concern for his well-being with the individual afterward, and also with the project leader, who then notifies the mental health staff at the institution.

In this discussion of Pongo's reporting policies, the issue is *immediate risk*. As an outside arts program, not employed by an agency or institution, Pongo does not consider itself a mandatory reporter that must report every disclosure by a youth of past abuse. Pongo focuses on the centerpiece of its mission, to help the youth express themselves creatively and freely about difficult experiences, including past abuse.

Issues of Safety in Groups

When working with groups of distressed teens in settings such as a juvenile detention center or a psychiatric hospital, the safety issues range from ensuring physical safety, to protecting confidentiality, to creating a respectful environment in which people feel comfortable enough to be open and creative. The particular challenge is to manage group dynamics so that people feel purposeful in the group, respectful of one another's issues, and personally safe. See chapter 14.

Issues of Mentor Safety

In terms of a mentor's physical safety, Pongo runs its projects in teams under the guidance of an experienced leader who knows the youth and the institution, and who is responsible for communication with the institution. All mentors work together, in one room, under the leader's direction. All mentors are trained before a project starts and then supported as they learn.

In addition, all mentors sign a Volunteer Agreement, which is discussed at the beginning of Pongo training. The agreement requires, among other things, that mentors not contact youth outside their Pongo responsibilities, that they not give out their personal information to a youth, that they follow all institutional rules, that they follow all Pongo policies, and that they maintain the highest ethical standards.

Obviously, Pongo's standards are a protection for the youth, as well as the mentors.

In terms of a mentor's emotional health, Pongo provides a poetry group for mentors at the beginning of each weekly session, and a wrap-up meeting at the end of each weekly session, at which mentors can discuss emotionally challenging experiences in their Pongo work, or emotionally challenging experiences outside Pongo that affect their feelings that day.

Issues of Program Safety

There is another safety necessity that is relevant to the Pongo program, especially within an institutional setting. Pongo has to be careful that a mentor's personality issues don't create dissension between Pongo and an institution, or within the Pongo program itself. In particular, Pongo monitors for the behavior of "splitting," in which a person might decide that there are good and bad individuals or groups, and form judgments and alliances on that basis. For example, it is not safe for a mentor to hold the belief that detention youth are good and the detention staff are bad, or vice versa, or take sides against leaders or others within Pongo. Such splitting is an opening for emotionally vulnerable people, such as Pongo's authors, to act out, in which they might argue with or threaten the individuals on one side of the split.

Pongo reserves the right to remove mentors from the program at any time and for any reason, without feeling a need to justify such a decision beyond a careful consideration that it is best for the program. There is too much at stake to do otherwise.

Issues of Safety in Publishing and the Website

For youth in the juvenile justice and social service systems, there are requirements that their confidentiality is maintained. It is Pongo's blanket policy to maintain confidentiality when it publishes, even in situations where confidentiality is not required. Though youth often want their real names attached to their poetry, Pongo feels an ethical responsibility to protect youth in this way. This topic is discussed in chapter 15.

Also, young people from all over the country send Pongo their poetry on the Pongo website. Sometimes a teen's poem will raise alarm about the teen's mental health or physical safety. Pongo has mentors assigned to write responses to every poem that is submitted. These mentors have found, from the young people's responses to their messages, that the writing is often a coping mechanism and, actually, a sign of resilience under these circumstances.

However, a mentor does respond honestly when she feels anxiety for a teen: The mentor will say that she is sorry if the teen's poem reflects a difficult personal experience. The mentor will reassure the teen that she is not alone. The mentor will mention the availability of crisis lines, where there are people ready to talk to the teen about her life. As always, the mentor communicates with the youth sincerely, but from her perspective as a poetry ally.

To support the ongoing use of writing for growth and healing, by all teens, including teens in crisis, the Pongo mentors praise every web author for her poetry, and encourage every web author to keep writing.

8

Introducing Poetry to Youth

Kaz
by a young gay man, age 20

All they see is the outer layer,
this façade, masquerade,
the <u>man</u> I should be by now.
BUT HIDDEN INSIDE IS STILL THE TERRIFIED, SILENT
<u>boy</u> WHO CAN'T GRASP THE WORLD AROUND HIM SO HE
MAKES A PRIVATE ONE INSIDE HIS HEAD.
This side,
my <u>Kaz</u>,
he should be gone by now.
He was supposed to have died
with all the painful, frightening memories.
But he's still here.
I MANAGE TO HIDE HIM FOR A WHILE, BUT HE ALWAYS
COMES BACK OUT AND UNKNOWINGLY CAUSES TROUBLE AND
HURTS HIMSELF AND OTHERS WITH HIS ACTIONS.
He's confused.
He's worried.
He runs and hides.

He's a paradox,
terrified of abandonment
yet content to live in silence.
I love him because
he is part of me,
I hate him for the same reason.

Teachers and counselors may wonder how to get started with poetry, in particular how to introduce poetry to youth in a way that encourages their enthusiastic involvement. They may worry that youth might be resistant, that youth might characterize poetry as weak. They may worry that some teens' poor language skills might cause them to shut down fearfully when asked to write. They may worry that youth would not support one another through any process that calls for personal openness.

All of these worries are completely understandable, of course, but it's Pongo's experience that youth who have led difficult lives are highly motivated to write, and take risks, once they feel safe in the process. They are naturally supportive of one another, too.

Purpose, Poetry, Patience, and Unexpected Outcomes

In 2002 I brought Pongo to a resource center for lesbian, gay, bisexual, transgender, and questioning youth. Many were homeless, having run away from home to escape rejection and violence in their families and communities. The center was open during the late afternoon on weekdays, when the youth would drop in, lower their packs, slouch on the couches, snack in the kitchen, and, especially, socialize. In good weather there were picnic tables out back.

In this context I talked to the teens individually to introduce poetry. I would circulate in the community, explain my purposes, share poetry, and invite the youth to write with me in that moment. I expressed the hope, without a guarantee, that we might publish a book. I asked if they wrote, and expressed interest in seeing or hearing their poetry. I was always supportive. I shared books of powerful teen writing that Pongo had published in the past.

I encouraged the youth to browse the books and tell me which poems they liked. One important topic, implied or stated, was that poetry could express deep and complicated feelings about difficult situations.

Mostly I expressed an interest in what the youth had to say about their lives. I shared Pongo's intention, that we want people to "Write from the heart about who you are as a person." My goal was always to bring new writers into the process, and I explained to youth that if they had never written before that I could help. The teens' truth was the most important outcome. I expressed my belief that "Honesty is the most important quality of good poetry."

When teens wrote with me or shared their work, I asked them to sign forms that gave me permission to publish (where publication was a possibility only). I typed up their work and gave them multiple copies to have and share. When I typed up the work, I corrected spelling and made grammar consistent, so that nothing would distract a reader from the teens' words. I preserved the teens' own voices and idiom.

As youth worked with me they saw that the process was respectful of them, and that it was easy and rewarding, while it helped them feel better. In this environment, more and more teens were eager to participate. The youth in the community were won over quickly.

Over time the teens wrote about their pride, accomplishment, and love. But also some wrote about drugs, prostitution, confusion, and the horror of witnessing degradation and death on the streets. They wrote about the simple challenges of being themselves in an often hostile world. A significant theme emerged, spontaneously, that the youth felt they were forced to wear masks because of their sexual and gender orientation.

It was an education to me when the theme of "masks" appeared again and again in the youth poetry. We eventually published a chapbook with the title "See What Goes on Behind My Masks." The poem that opens this chapter, "Kaz," was included in this book.

It is important to understand that there was a flow to this process over the weeks, a process during which more and more personal writing was gathered from more and more participants, but where some days resulted in fewer connections and fewer satisfactory interactions than others. I was patient, but persistent. I was encouraging, but not controlling. I did my best to build relationships. I respected the teens' need to feel in control. The basis of my interest was that I honored the young people's voices, which they understood.

If someone didn't want to work with me on a particular day, I asked if she would consider working with me the next week. If no one wanted to work with me, I'd hang out in the kitchen and play cards or read poetry.

As the writing program went on, there were unexpected connections and poems.

One transgender youth rejected my regular requests that she write with me. She insisted that she never wrote poetry. Then one day, about four months later, she came in to the center looking for me, to proudly hand me a spiral notebook filled with her writing.

Another youth never wanted to write. I got to know him a little, and one day, very uncharacteristically for me, I grabbed his arm and said, "OK. Enough. Today you write with me." We were beginning our work, sitting next to each other in the living room, when one of the young man's friends asked him to step outside for a cigarette. My author said, "I can't. He's making me write a poem." The young man dictated a poem about rejection at home, and about a life on the streets that included drugs and prostitution.

Purpose and Poetry with Groups

In introducing poetry to groups, the principles are the same as those used in the anecdote above. In front of a group, Pongo mentors will explain the Pongo history and intention. They will ask people to "Write from the heart about who you are as a person." They will talk about the possibility of publication. They will share poetry that is meaningful to the young people's lives. They will ask about people's own poetry, and invite them to share. They will talk about the ability of poetry to convey complicated experiences and feelings. They will assure young people that the Pongo mentors can help those who haven't written before.

One time I was talking to a class at juvenile detention, in preparation for taking volunteers out of class to write. There was a substitute teacher that day, and the classroom atmosphere felt unsafe. One large and muscular seventeen-year-old was bullying and manipulating the group, often through his cohorts. People were afraid to speak. I recognized aloud that poetry might not be an option that day, but I talked about my interest in poetry and shared some poems on difficult themes, including physical abuse. I read one poem that mentioned an author's worry for his brother in their abusive home. (Worry about siblings is a significant theme in teens' writing about abusive situations.)

The young man who had been manipulating the group looked up at me. He said, "I remember you. You published a poem by my twin brother." I remembered. I had published the poem four years before, when the twins were in detention, and they were small, thin, and babyish in appearance. The brother's poem was about dealing drugs and carrying a gun at thirteen years old in order to support his family

The tone in the group changed. The seventeen-year-old joined Pongo to write that day.

Finding Poetry to Share

An important way that Pongo introduces poetry writing to distressed youth is by sharing poems that move and inspire them, poems that speak to the teens' difficult experiences, representing emotions that are often unarticulated in their lives.

There are hundreds of these poems on the Pongo website, by the Pongo authors, and they may be shared in classrooms. There are hundreds of these poems that have been published in Pongo books, and some of these books are available from the website. In addition there are great books of teen writing, such as the books by WritersCorps, which is an alliance of creative writing programs in San Francisco, the Bronx, and Washington, DC.

Also, there are many published anthologies of poems, both by established and new poets, that are based on emotional themes. Anthology subjects include father-daughter poems, mother poems, poems after a death, poems about women in love, poems by wives after divorce, poems by children after divorce, poems by immigrants, poems about domestic violence, poems about mental illness, poems about the stages and relationships in the lives of men, poems about addiction, poems about the Native American experience, poems about the African American experience, poems about the LGBT experience, etc. Many anthologies are out of print, but they can be found in libraries or purchased used. There is a list of anthologies on the Pongo website. Some of the poems in these anthologies can also serve as models for new writing activities, too.

The Messages That Help Bring Youth to Poetry

To introduce poetry to youth, and draw them into a process that includes openness (and risk), there are particular messages that the Pongo mentors convey through specific words and actions. For Pongo, these messages are at the heart of the program culture. Pongo asks its mentors to memorize these words and use them literally. Table 8.1 summarizes some of the key messages, followed by the words and/or actions that communicate them.

Table 8.1. Key Messages and Words/Actions That Support Messages

Key Messages	Words and Actions That Support Messages
We are interested in you and your life.	Words: "We ask you to 'Write from the heart about who you are as a person.'"
We are interested in truthfulness and not in judging you for correctness.	Words: "Honesty is the most important quality of good writing."
We believe in the value of what you have to communicate.	Action: This message is communicated through our interest in sharing youth writing with others (perhaps through publication, readings, posting).
We can handle, and will welcome, your feelings.	Action: This message is communicated in our willingness to read poetry on emotionally relevant themes—especially poetry by other youth.
We respect your truth.	Words: "We believe that people who've had difficult experiences have important things to say."
We will be strong for safety.	Words and Action: This message is primarily communicated through our mature ability to listen to painful stories without needing to turn away or reject feeling. It is also represented during group work through our ability to set high expectations while effectively responding to unproductive group dynamics. We might say at the start of every group, "We strive to keep this a safe place."
We will protect your confidentiality.	Words and Action: We have a clear policy that we will not use real names, and we do not share youth writing, in a classroom or publication, without youth permission.
We must report situations in which you or someone you know is in imminent danger.	Words and Action: At the beginning of the writing session, we show youth a statement, which says we will want to talk to them and act responsibly, if we think they, or someone they know, is at imminent risk.
We believe that your writing has a social purpose.	Words: "We think your writing can help other youth, and can help adults to understand teens better."

(*continued*)

Table 8.1. (*continued*)

Key Messages	Words and Actions That Support Messages
We are interested in your truth, not in correcting your technique.	Words: "Don't worry about spelling and grammar. We'll help you fix that."
We are interested in what you've written.	Words: "Does anyone in this group write poetry? Do you have a poem you're willing to share right now?"
We would like to work with inexperienced poets, and we are confident in our ability to help.	Words and Action: We don't seek writers by asking, "Who wants to write poetry with us?" Instead, we ask, "Who hasn't written poetry before?" With the Pongo Method, we provide new writers with a successful writing experience.
We don't want you to feel pressured to write.	Words: "Just give it a try. Do your best. We can help. We know that writing poetry is hard."
We are comfortable giving you control in this process.	Words: "If you really don't want to work with us today, that's OK. Will you think about working with us next week?"
You have control over what you say and what happens to it.	Words: "I may offer ideas or make suggestions, but I want you to know that this is your poem, and the decisions are yours. Also, you own your poem, and it's your decision whether or not your poem is shared with anyone else."
We will not overpromise when it comes to publication.	Words: "We try very hard not to make promises that we can't keep. We don't know whether or not we will publish your poem eventually. There are a lot of reasons why a poem might not be chosen for publication that have nothing to do with the quality of the poem. Making a book is like making a poem, things have to fit together and flow effectively."
You can do this, what you write is important, and we believe in you.	Words: "You did great work today. I hope you keep writing!"

9

Overview of the One-on-One Process

Doors of Emotion
by a young woman in juvenile detention, age 15

I'm opening up closed doors
Behind one door I find sadness
It's blue, it's boring, it's lonely, it makes you cry

Behind another door
You see happy people enjoying things they like
You hate them because they're happy, and you're not
So you slam the door and move to the next one

The next door is terrifying
You see guns and drugs and people dying
It's a dangerous door to walk through

There's a door in my heart
It's so full that when you open it
Everything comes tumbling down
All the frustrations, the joys, the hate, the love

Somewhere in there is the perfect life
A perfect me

This is a great moment, when an adult mentor first sits down with a teen to help her write personal poetry. There is a significant chance that, following the Pongo Method, the adult and the teen will share a surprising, deeply moving, life-changing, and also joyful experience.

In the Pongo Method, the adult is actively involved in the writing process along with the youth, offering writing structures and poetic techniques, asking questions, but always with a certain humility. The adult supports a level of control for the young writers that keeps the process safe.

As the adult works with a teen, he will thoughtfully choose a writing mode for the teen's work, or a series of different modes. These choices are to determine whether

1. a teen writes independently, *or*
2. the adult takes dictation in a structured but free-flowing technique, *or*
3. the adult improvises a poem structure in the moment, based on an easy and appealing topic, such as wishes, lists, an emotion, a chronology, etc., *or*
4. the adult provides a highly structured activity such as a fill-in-the-blank poem on a relevant theme for the teen.

With these writing modes, *every teen can write a poem in every one-on-one writing session.*

As You Begin Working with Youth

The Pongo philosophy is to provide as much structure, but also as little structure, as a youth needs in order to write freely. A Pongo mentor is always providing options, offering suggestions, demonstrating poetic techniques, and reacting responsively, in a way that supports and enhances the teen's writing process. The following scenarios demonstrate how a mentor chooses a poetic mode.

Scenario One: Taking Dictation
The mentor just sat down with a teen, and he wants to move into an appropriately supportive process to help the youth write a personal poem. Here is one possible discussion:

"Hi. Have a seat. My name is Richard. What's your name? . . . So you heard my introduction to your class. We ask writers to 'Write from the heart about who you are as a person.' Here's a book of teen poetry from here in juvie. You can keep it if you want. Maybe you'd like to browse through it and see what other teens here have written." [Teen browses book and reads a few poems.]

"Did you see a poem you liked? Which one? Yes, that is a good poem. It's great that people can write poetry about anything, even complicated experiences. Have you written poetry before?" [Teen: "Not really."]

"Good. This will be fun. Some teens want to write on their own, and that's fine. I have a pad and pencil for you. But most teens work with me. They talk about stuff, and I write it down, and we turn it into a poem together. Want to do that?" [Teen: "Yes."]

"OK. I'm writing your name and date. [Richard is writing on a pad or at a computer.] Now, is there anything on your mind today?" [Richard begins the process of taking dictation. This process is explained in chapter 10.]

Scenario Two: Improvising a Poetic Structure

A teen may get stuck in the process of writing on his own, or may have difficulty focusing on a particular feeling or experience in his dictated writing. Sometimes a mentor can hear enough from the teen to identify a particular issue that seems significant. With this information the mentor can improvise a poetic structure on a significant issue. In this process, a mentor may offer a number of ideas before she and the youth are inspired by one that works. This process calls on the mentor's own sensitivity and creativity, as in the following example:

"I'm getting some ideas for a poem we could work on now, if you want. You mentioned you were mad at your mom for not visiting you in detention. So we could write a poem about your mom. Sometimes people's relations with their family are complicated, there are things they love and things that make them mad. We could write about both. Or maybe, if anger is a big thing in your life, we could write about that, like we could list the things that make you angry, or a memory of a time when you were angry. Or maybe we could write about how you hope things will go for you with your mom when you get out of this place." [Richard watches the teen for reactions as choices are mentioned. He asks the teen if there is something she wants to write. Often a youth will say something that serves as a clue or an opening to what she needs to write. For example, suppose the teen says, "My anger is kind of out of control."]

"Wow, that would be a great topic to write about. Why don't we write a poem where there is a repeating refrain 'My anger is out of control.' Look, give me one example where your anger was out of control."

[As the teen talks, Richard writes down her words, followed by the line "My anger is out of control." He reads it back to the youth.] "Now give me another example." [The poem continues in this way, with incidents listed, while using a repeated refrain. This process is explained further in chapter 11.]

Scenario Three: Using a Fill-in-the-Blank Activity

Often in a thirty-minute session, a mentor has the opportunity to write several poems with a youth. This helps the mentor meet a significant goal of the Pongo Method, to guide the process so that it becomes more poetic and more personal as the writing session progresses, both within a poem and with each poem written. In this scenario a teen has chosen to write on his own, but he has written a poem that focuses on rhyme and that is not very personal. Of course, the mentor would always identify things he likes in that first poem, and offer sincere praise. The mentor might respond as follows:

"This is great. I like the way you repeated this line at the beginning and end. And I particularly liked this rhyme here. So we have time to write another poem. May I show you something?" [Richard goes to get a binder of Pongo fill-in-the-blank writing activities. (The activities are available for free download on the Pongo website.)]

"These are easy and fun to do. See each activity begins with an example poem here, then you just fill in the blanks. And you and I can do it together, if you want. Why don't you check these out."

[Then Richard opens the binder to the table of contents. The table of contents has the activity titles, which are evocative and might include "Addicted," "Running," "Lessons of Courage and Fear," "You Don't Know Me," etc.]

[The teen begins looking down the list in the table of contents, and then flipping to look at the individual activities. If the teen finds an interesting activity, he is encouraged to remove it from the binder and then complete it, either working on his own or working with Richard, who reads the activity prompts aloud and writes down the teen's responses in the blanks. This process is explained further in chapter 12.]

The Process for Choosing a Writing Mode

The scenarios above are examples of a process in which a writing mentor selects a writing mode that best meets an individual writer's need for creative and emotional support, at that moment. This support might come in the form of companionship, a helpful collaboration, a suggestive theme, an easy-to-complete (but personal) writing activity, etc. This selection of a writing mode is strategic, and is therefore described as a "drilldown" process, which is summarized in figure 9.1: "Pongo's Drilldown Process."

Issues with Teens Writing Independently

Some teens write brilliant, original poems on their own, poems that could never be replicated in a collaborative process. Some teens achieve this brilliance in the very first poem of their lives. As mentioned, Pongo's basic goal is to provide as much support, but also as little support, as a teen needs to write creatively.

But there are other times when young people working on their own will create poems that emphasize rhyme over personal content, or that represent stereotypical and destructive themes, such as poems that glorify street life or that celebrate an abusive boyfriend.

Such poems are not doing the essential work of Pongo, which is to facilitate and teach a personal poetry that speaks to a deeper truth, and that empowers people to understand their feelings and take better control over their lives. For example, though sometimes teens write about their drug use as fun (often when showing off in a group situation), the more fully realized poetry about drugs includes more complicated themes, such as how drug use can undermine the love in a family and how drug use can be a response to personal pain.

PONGO'S DRILLDOWN PROCESS

The information below summarizes Pongo's "drilldown process" for selecting a writing mode that a mentor will use with a particular youth one-on-one. Pongo calls this a drilldown process because the techniques are applied strategically, in response to a young person's particular needs.

Step	Writing First Poem	Choice of Technique
1	When you sit down with a youth, explain that you can work together in many different ways. Evaluate whether or not the youth is ready to write independently, or if he would like to dictate to you, or if he is completely at a loss where to begin.	
2	If teen is ready to write on his own…	Give the teen a pad and pen. Sit next to teen while he writes. Read or write yourself. Answer questions. Check in. Offer support. Be ready to help with a follow up poem.
3	If teen would like to dictate a poem…	Ask if teen has something on his mind. Respond quickly, starting dictation using the teen's preliminary comments. Follow *Taking Dictation* technique, which may evolve into *Improvising a Poetic Structure.*
4	If teen is in a particular emotional state or expresses specific issues, but has difficulty beginning…	Follow the technique *Improvising a Poetic Structure.* For example, if a teen is worried about an upcoming court appearance, you could improvise a poem about what it's like to feel worried, or a poem that imagines what might happen in court.
5	If a teen is unemotional and unclear where to begin…	Follow the technique *Using a Fill-in-the-Blank Activity.* Collaborate with the teen on this activity, helping him make choices, as necessary, and reading back to him his completed work.

FIGURE 9.1
Pongo's Drilldown Process

Step	Writing Second Poem	Choice of Technique
6	For this next piece of writing in a writing session, you will want to consciously move toward more personal writing (without being intrusive) and toward a more poetic experience…	
7	If the teen's first writing was original, personal, poetic…	Continue in a similar way for the second poem.
8	If the teen's first writing was stereotypical, superficial, or not helpful…	Suggest a different approach for the second poem. Encourage teen to "Write from the heart about who you are as a person." The new technique may be *Taking Dictation* or it may be *Improvising a Poetic Structure*. If you are improvising a poetic structure, look for personal themes that emerged in the first piece of writing or through conversation with the teen.
9	If you improvised a poetic structure for the first poem, and it was successful…	Try doing it again and *Improvising a Poetic Structure* for the next poem.
10	If you used a fill-in-the-blank poem for the first poem…	See if the youth now would like to write on his own, or if he has something on his mind that he would like to dictate to you.
11	If now, or at any point, you are at a loss for what to do next…	Follow the technique *Using a Fill-in-the-Blank Poem*. Collaborate with the teen on this activity, helping him make choices, as necessary, and reading back to him his completed work.

FIGURE 9.1
(*continued*)

There are times when a writing mentor will want to guide a youth away from independent writing in order to provide a structured experience that teaches the young person how to use personal reflection when writing poetry. This structured experience might be provided by a Pongo fill-in-the-blank poem.

Setting Limits on Content

The Pongo Method includes acceptance of teen poems and praise for the effort, but there are times when limits must be set on what a teen can write. For example, one time a young man in detention, who had a profound emotional problem, started to dictate sexually explicit material to a female Pongo mentor. It was correctly recognized as inappropriate, and when the writing mentors discussed the situation with their contacts on the staff, the mentors found out that the teen had already been given warnings and restrictions because of this behavior.

The Pongo mentors also feel comfortable setting limits on misogynistic content, which is sometimes a regrettable societal theme. Mentors can respond by speaking honestly and expressing their discomfort, and then redirecting the writer to write something more personal. A mentor can make this point in a way that sets an important example of humane values, yet still expresses interest in the youth.

Similarly, teens sometimes write about violence in a cinematic, impersonal way, based on cultural models. The writing mentor might redirect this writing by saying: "This is OK, but frankly, a lot of different people could write something like this. We're really more interested in you, what your life is like, what's in your heart." The teens understand the mentor's intention, and respond.

Sometimes teens use obscenity in their writing, which the Pongo mentors don't necessarily object to (when it's expressed honestly), but which is against the rules inside juvenile detention. A mentor will simply remind the teen of the rule against obscenity and ask the youth if he can't come up with an alternative way of expressing himself. Finding an alternative is never a problem.

10

Taking Dictation

Earliest Memories
by a young man in juvenile detention, age 12(?)

I remember when I was young
I used to live with a lady, my aunt named Judy,
with my mom in a drug house,
a white house with messed up steps
You walked in, there were kids all running around
in Pampers, no shirts, garbage all over,
Kentucky Fried Chicken boxes all over the place,
blood splattered all over the wall,
dirty kitchen, dirty dishes all in the kitchen,
all you see around was
pimps, hustlers, young gang members,
teenage girls,
people running in and out at all hours of the night,
always making noise, people always fighting,
all you see is money, people chopping up dope

At the time I was young, I was 6,
I was seeing all this

thinking that I wanted to be
the youngest pimp alive,
let alone that it was all around me,
I was trapped,
it was all around me, there,
it was over my friend's house,
everywhere, it was just like that
I was trapped in the ghetto

The *Taking Dictation* technique is Pongo's core method for facilitating poetry one-on-one with teens who have suffered trauma. The technique helps youth talk about things they've never talked about before. To achieve this result, the Pongo mentors apply all that they've learned about the writing mentor's special role with a youth, to be a caring and patient listener and a skilled poetry facilitator. The mentor guides the *Taking Dictation* process by asking questions, making suggestions, offering praise, and leaving ultimate control over the poem in the hands of the teen. The *Taking Dictation* process is explained with a specific set of directions below, and it is illustrated in a "scenario" later in the chapter.

Directions for Taking Dictation

The following directions are addressed to a mentor who is about to use the *Taking Dictation* technique with a teen. The mentor is already sitting with a teen, after introducing poetry and the Pongo intentions. The mentor has a pad in hand or is sitting at a computer, ready to write. These directions tell the mentor how to begin and proceed, and they include some general intentions that the mentor needs to keep in mind throughout the writing process.

1. To begin, ask the teen, "Is there anything on your mind today?"
2. Write down the first thing the teen says. Don't worry if it seems banal or unpoetic. Ask for clarification. For example, if a teen says she's sleepy, you might ask if it's hard for her to sleep lately, or if she'd rather be asleep than awake right now. This might lead to discussion about the teen missing her

bed, or about the teen worrying about her family, or about the teen not wanting to feel *anything* anymore.

3. As you and the teen talk, write down the content as you go. Don't sit there listening without writing. Your goal is to capture the teen's actual words, her voice in the dialogue. Immediacy is important. Great meaning is conveyed in what and how a teen expresses herself. The one alteration you should make is that you should try to write the teen's words in the form of poetic lines—sentence fragments that use line breaks to capture the rhythms of the teen's breath and thoughts. This rhythm captures significant emotional content.

4. One of the mistakes that new mentors make, in the beginning, is to write down the content that represents a story's outline, but leave out the teen's asides, doubts, anecdotes, and feelings that reveal a deeper, more personal truth. For example if a teen is talking about her current drug usage, but laughs awkwardly and says that the first time she used drugs was with her mom at age ten, this aside is a significant part of the story and needs to be written down. You should listen for significant details that are spoken parenthetically.

5. One of the challenges you may face at the beginning of a writing session is a teen's expectation and desire to rhyme. It's best to discourage this, kindly, by explaining that poetry doesn't have to rhyme, and that in fact rhyming can get in the way of speaking about important things. Some youth won't be deterred from rhyming, and so that will be the poem you facilitate.

6. *General Intention*: Once the writing process is under way, the mentor's most significant goals are to help the teen's writing become *more personal* and *more poetic*. This is achieved through suggestions, as necessary, that the teen include feelings, memories, poetic images (metaphors and similes), sensory images, etc. (IMPORTANT: Please refer to figure 10.1, "Pongo Teen Writing: Ideas for Personal Content and Poetic Enhancement." Pongo uses this one-page document as a "cheat sheet," a resource that a mentor can have beside her, for ideas, while working with a teen. This document was created by Pongo leader Adrienne Johanson.)

7. One of your great assets as a facilitator of the teen's poem is that you represent the audience. You are essentially the "reader" of the teen's poem as it is written. You can respond and make suggestions, not as a critic but as a fan. At any point you can say, "This is great, but I'm curious how you

felt when that happened. I think it would be very interesting for a reader if you add that here."

8. And when you do relate to the teen as a teacher, for example in explaining how to include a simile in her poem, it is explained in the context of an opportunity—as in, "You know what would be cool here? You could add a simile. Do you know what that is? For example, when you say you're angry, you could write it as 'I'm as angry as a tornado that could knock a house down' or 'I'm as angry as a shark when it attacks.' Want to try a simile?" Note also that your principal method as a teacher, for instance as a teacher of simile, is to provide examples. It is the examples that stimulate the teen's easy creativity and reinforce the enjoyable collaborative process that you and the teen share.

9. It is very important that you read the teen's poem back to her periodically throughout the process. For example, you might read the entire poem to the teen after each stanza is added. In this way you are doing several things: You are reinforcing the value of the teen's words, you are representing your own pleasure in her work, and you are stimulating her next creative ideas. It's a lot easier for the teen to write line seventeen of a poem if she has just heard the sixteen lines that precede it, and is thereby immersed in the poem's context, tone, and flow. When a teen hears her work read aloud, she is often surprised and pleased to discover what she has accomplished. There is often a special moment at the end of a session when you read a teen's entire poem aloud and see the pleasure on her face.

10. As suggested above (in the specific context of teaching simile), you should provide lots of examples and ideas during the writing process. For example, if a teen has written that his mom walked out on him, you might say, "That must have been awful for you. Do you want to say in your poem how you felt? Like maybe you were angry or upset or numb. Maybe you felt afraid. Want to say something about that here?" Your ideas stimulate the teen's own words. You don't need to worry that your ideas will determine in an unnatural way what the teen writes. Any writer is inspired by others' ideas to think of his own.

11. *General Intention*: You are always honoring the fact that the poem belongs to the teen, and he retains control. In other words, your suggestions are merely suggestions. A teen may choose to use them or not. In this way you keep the writing process safe, which in turn frees the teen to feel both

positive about working with you and more open. Ultimately, the teen also controls whether or not her poem is shared, or even saved.

12. Teens will sometimes write on topics that do not explore their emotional selves. For example, they may gripe about detention rather than explore the betrayals, loss, and anger that led them into street life and later arrest. The move toward more personal writing is described as a process, one that is not always achievable, but one that is always encouraged when it's timely.

13. In addition, you should know that personal writing for victims of trauma is not universally sad. Many teens will celebrate their love for siblings, pets, special people, special times, and special places. Many teens will write about values and aspirations for their future, especially with your guidance, as discussed below. These positive topics are important forms of personal writing and are affirmations of hope and resilience for trauma victims.

14. It is important to give the teen writer your focused attention and to offer sincere praise during the writing process. Your praise may take the form of appreciation for a word choice, a unique effort, or a courageous attempt to write on a difficult topic.

15. An essential quality of poetry is that it moves toward a transformative moment at the end, a moment of resolution, articulation, or insight. You will find as you take dictation that, if you help the teen remain focused, *the emotional truth will deepen as you go along.* You should facilitate a powerful conclusion by alerting the teen to the ending, for instance by asking a teen for "one last example" or by asking a teen how she'd like to end her poem.

16. Because the ending of a poem has a powerful emotional residue, there is a particular choice for you to make as a facilitator. If a poem is about a sad topic, such as a teen's sense of loss and betrayal after being abused as a child, you can provide opportunities for a resilient ending. Such endings may be in the form of facilitating a teen's expressions of principle, such as how the teen would treat her own child differently, or facilitating a vision of a better world, such as the teen's wish for a world in which all children receive only love. The resilient ending might also mention a teen's personal resilient qualities. (See table 10.1, "Resilient Qualities of Young Writers.")

17. A mentor's decision about whether or not to suggest a resilient ending for a poem can be determined by a mentor's intuition about a young person's vulnerability. Do you think a teen needs a way out of sadness, needs something positive to cling to in the moment? For a mentor who is unsure what to do in response to a teen's sadness, especially for a new mentor at the beginning of learning the Pongo Method, it is best to err on the side of everyone's comfort, and offer opportunities for hope and resilience to a teen at a poem's end. You can help a teen write about her wishes, resources, principles, aspirations, and strengths.

18. The time to name a poem (or rename a poem) may come when the poem is done, and you read the entire poem aloud to the teen. That's when you might ask, "What would you like to title your poem?" As always, you can offer your own ideas as suggestions. You and the teen will probably have similar ideas for a title.

19. When you follow the Pongo approach, you will provide an opportunity for the teen to share her poem after it is written, if possible, probably with other teens and mentors who are writing that day. The teen may prefer that *you* read her poem aloud to the group for her. You should realize that it is important to have the teen's permission to share her work, and that there are issues associated with sharing, including a poem's appropriateness for its audience.

PONGO TEEN WRITING PROJECT

Ideas for Personal Content and Poetic Enhancements

Repeated words ....softly Softly........... ......softly......	**Repeated lines** That's when I feel the thunder inside .... That's why I feel the thunder inside
Metaphors *(image used to represent something else)* "I am not the apple of anyone's eye. I am the strange kumquat Caught between A grape and a tangerine. I'm the last fruit in the basket, Because no one knows what to do With me."	**Similes** *(something is "like" or "as" something else)* "Your kindness is a constant surprise, Like the river passing through Wright's *Fallingwater*. Life can be so loud that I'm sure it's dwellers sometimes forgot The rushing water under their feet."
Wishes I wish I had a million dollars, I'd buy... I wish there was peace... I wish I could understand...	**Emotions** The events, times, people, that make me feel joyful or fearful or ??? (Emotions might include joy, trust, fear, surprise, sadness, disgust, anger, anticipation)
Lists The things I'd like to change... The things I've learned about people... Pictures of my home...	**Memories** I remember the first time... I remember the last time... I remember the kitchen table...
Senses *(Sight, sound, touch, hearing, smell,* *taste...)* What are the sounds of your street? Tastes of your home? Sights of summer?	**Questions** *(Who, what, when, where, why...)* List your questions about life, about adulthood, about love, about death
Good/Bad Good about mothers, bad about mothers. Good about ???, bad about ???	**What-If** What if alcohol had never been invented? What if people had warning lights?

FIGURE 10.1

Pongo Teen Writing: Ideas for Personal Content and Poetic Enhancement

Table 10.1. Resilient Qualities of Young Writers

Here are some of the resilient qualities that many Pongo teen writers possess, and that they can be praised for and helped to include in their writing. Distressed youth are often...

Caring	Intelligent	Courageous	Determined
Honest	Loyal	Compassionate	Proud
Hopeful	Loving	Helpful	Creative
Sensitive	Resourceful	Funny	Emotional

"Taking Dictation" Scenario

The following scenario depicts a dialogue between a mentor and a teen writer, during the process of *Taking Dictation*:

Richard, the Pongo writing mentor [after introducing Pongo, and sharing poetry examples, and deciding with the teen to take dictation]: Anything on your mind today?

Teen: Not really . . . I'm pretty bored.

R: OK, I'm writing "I'm pretty bored right now." How come?

T: I guess I don't want to think about stuff.

R: Good. "I don't want to think about stuff." Like what?

T: Like what my brother's doing right now.

R: Why is that?

T: Because he looks up to me and is following in my footsteps.

R: Like with gangs or drugs or something?

T: Yes. He's involved in a gang.

R: OK. This is what I have so far. "I'm pretty bored right now. / Don't want to think about stuff. / Like what my brother is doing right now. / He looks up to me and is following in my footsteps, / Joining a gang." How does that sound?

T: Good.

R: OK, we have the option now of writing more about your brother, or maybe listing some other things you don't want to think about.

T: Other things.

R: Like?

T: I don't know. My mom . . . my future . . . my dad . . . what's going to happen when I get out.

R: Great. That will make a great poem. OK, before we go on, I have a suggestion to make. We could use a poetic image here, if you want. For example, what does it feel like when you think about your brother, is it a burning feeling like sitting too close to a fire, is it an icy feeling like snow down your back—?

T: It's like feeling afraid, like helpless, like having a mountain falling on you.

R: That's great. This is a terrific beginning. Good, here's what I've written down so far. *[Reads first stanza with addition of lines "I feel afraid, like helpless, / Like having a mountain falling on me"]* How does that sound? Do you like it? Want to change anything? *[T. shakes head "no."]* Now your mom. I'm beginning your next stanza with the line "I don't want to think about my mom." Why?

T: She doesn't want me to be here. I told her I wouldn't end up here again.

R: Great. I've got that down. Are you worried about how your being here affects her? Or maybe worried that she'll love you less? Or something else?

T: Sort of. I think she's had a lot of trouble in her life, and I'm making things worse.

R: OK so this is what I've written. "I don't want to think about my mom. / She doesn't want me to be here. / And I told her I wouldn't end up here again. / She's had a lot of trouble in her life, / And I'm making things worse." Great. Sound good to you? Now, how about a poetic image. Thinking about your mom is like . . . what?

T: I feel like I'm the leaky roof over her head.

R: Beautiful. Now your dad. You said he is someone you don't want to think about, too. Why?

T: I don't want to think about the fact that my dad used to beat us.

R: You mean he beat you, your mom, and your brother? Do you want to say how it affected you?

T: Like it made me angry all the time.

R: How has the anger expressed itself? You get into fights? Or rebel? Or something else?

T: Yes, and I always get impatient with people. Sometimes I use drugs to calm me down.

R: Got it. How about another simile? When I think of my dad I feel like . . . what?

T: I feel like I'm on fire.

R: Great. You know, a long time ago, people used to think the world was made up of four elements: earth, air, fire, and water. It happens that your three images represent three of those. The mountain is earth, the leaks are water, and now fire. Maybe your last image could be an air image. Then your poem could be the four elements. It's up to you. Just something that occurred to me. Shall I read what you have so far? [Richard reads entire poem including third stanza: "I don't want to think about my dad, / How he used to beat us. / It makes me angry all the time. / Now I'm impatient with people, / And I have to use drugs sometimes to calm down. / I feel like I'm on fire."] Sound OK? Want to change anything?

T: [Shakes his head "no."]

R: OK. The last thing you mentioned is that you don't want to think about your future. That would be a good way to end your poem, too. Does that sound good? What is it that you don't want to think about, in terms of your future?

T: I'm wondering if I can change anything. Like what kind of man will I be. Will I be like my dad?

R: What kind of man would you like to be?

T: I'd like to be someone who takes care of my family, has a job, doesn't get in trouble.

R: How would that make you feel?

T: Like a fresh breeze.

R: Wow. That's great. You did create an air image. Do you want to call your poem "The Four Elements"?

T: How about "The Elements of Me"?

R: That's great. Let me read the whole thing back to you. You did a terrific job. You tell me if there's anything you want to change:

The Elements of Me

I'm pretty bored right now.
Don't want to think about stuff.
Like what my brother is doing right now.
He looks up to me and is following in my footsteps,
joining a gang.
I feel afraid, helpless,
like having a mountain falling on me.

I don't want to think about my mom.
She doesn't want me to be here.
I told her I wouldn't end up here again.
She's had a lot of trouble in her life,
and I'm making things worse.
I feel like I'm the leaky roof over her head.

I don't want to think about my dad,
how he used to beat us
It makes me angry all the time.
Now I'm impatient with people,
and I have to use drugs sometimes to calm down.
I feel like I'm on fire.

I don't want to think about my future.
I'm wondering if I can change anything,
like what kind of man I will be.
Will I be like my dad?
I'd like to be someone who takes care of my family,
has a job, doesn't get into trouble.
If I could do that I'd feel like
a fresh breeze.

11

Improvising Poetic Structures

Wish Poem
by a young man in a center for homeless youth, age 13(?)

I wish I had
a thousand dollars
I'd buy a lot of candy
Jolly Ranchers, gum, Daffy Taffys,
Airheads, Tootsie Rolls, Snickers,
Milky Ways, Skittles, M&Ms,
Mombas, KitKats, sodas

I'd be the Candy King
My country would be all chocolate
You could take a bite out of crime
You could bite the police
There'd be chocolate fires you could eat
There'd be chocolate flowers you could eat
My chocolate land would be bad
There be bad people with 22s, machine guns,
shooting the chocolate police

But I'm the Candy King
I'd just tell the police to leave
my chocolate land

In the Pongo Method, a writing mentor has a wonderful opportunity to utilize his own creativity during a one-on-one writing session with a youth. The mentor can improvise a poetic structure (make an inspired suggestion of a poetic form for a teen's poem) that helps the teen express and understand her difficult and complicated emotions.

The writing mode of *Improvising a Poetic Structure* is different from the mode of *Taking Dictation* in that a mentor who is *Taking Dictation* begins with a teen's narrative, and helps to make that narrative poetic. A mentor who is *Taking Dictation* will ask a youth, "Is there anything on your mind today?" and then request elaboration, while helping the teen to express herself more poetically by facilitating line breaks, repetition, poetic imagery, etc. The mentor will also help the teen to express herself more poetically by encouraging more emotional openness through greater expression of feelings, memories, and sensory images.

These same skills apply when *Improvising a Poetic Structure*, except that in this mode the mentor is also suggesting a poetic form for the teen's poem, moving from articulating a poetic narrative to creating a focused Wish Poem, List Poem, Memory Poem, Emotion Poem, etc.

Sometimes the choice of a form is direct and natural, a literal reflection of what a teen is talking about—a wish, a memory, an emotion. For example, if a teen first writes a poem that angrily describes her frustration with detention, the mentor might suggest that the teen write an Emotion Poem next, about her anger.

Sometimes the choice of a form is an inspired and creative suggestion by a mentor, based on what a teen has difficulty discussing. For example, if a teen struggles to come up with an idea for a first poem, the mentor might suggest that the teen write a Wish Poem, in which she imagines happy dreams and possibilities.

Sometimes the choice of a form is a request to focus on a particular technique, such as a Repeated Line Poem or a Poetic Image Poem. This might be an inspired suggestion by a mentor based on a teen's resonant words or imagination.

While the creative opportunities of improvisation are, of course, limitless, the Pongo Method proposes a foundation of ten forms for improvisation because they are consistently effective with distressed youth. These forms provide a framework for expressing the young people's life experience, hopes, strong emotions, complicated emotions, and reflections.

The ten forms, such as the Wish Poem, are so effective, in fact, that they can guarantee a creative outcome every time a writing mentor sits down with a youth. Every teen can be helped to write a Wish Poem.

These forms, listed below, are all referenced generally on Pongo's "cheat sheet," a one-page summary of creative ideas that a mentor can have beside her as she works with a teen. (The cheat sheet is a resource whether a mentor is *Taking Dictation* or *Improvising a Poetic Structure*.) The cheat sheet is called "Pongo Teen Writing: Ideas for Personal Content and Poetic Enhancement" and is included in the previous chapter.

Ten Forms for Improvised Poems

The ten forms for *Improvising a Poetic Structure* are listed below with examples from my own work, and that of other Pongo writing mentors, with different youth.

Wish Poem

One poetic structure that can always be guided to completion is a Wish Poem (Koch 1971). This poem begins with the title "Wish Poem" and has a first line of "I wish." Then the mentor asks a teen what she would wish for. If a teen has a hard time talking, the mentor might ask questions and make suggestions that become increasingly specific, as necessary:

What would you wish for? (A thousand dollars.)

What would you buy with the money? (A lot of candy)

What kinds of candy? (Jolly Ranchers, etc.)

Maybe you'd like to be the Candy King. (Yes)

Would your kingdom be made of candy?

What would your kingdom be like?

In this technique, the mentor would write down the teen's words, allowing for collaborations, to create a poem. In the example from the opening poem of this chapter, I was working with a small and nervous boy in a center for homeless youth. He was very distracted and afraid, so I helped the youth with an imaginative suggestion that maybe he could be the Candy King in his own Candy Land:

Wish Poem
by a young man in a center for homeless youth, age 13(?)

I wish I had a thousand dollars
I'd buy a lot of candy
Jolly Ranchers, gum, Daffy Taffys,
Airheads, Tootsie Rolls, Snickers,
Milky Ways, Skittles, M&Ms,
Mombas, KitKats, sodas,

I'd be the Candy King
My country would be all chocolate

In the case of this Wish Poem, which describes a Candy Land, the boy started to write about chocolate gangsters and chocolate policemen who were shooting one another. He could not extricate himself from a disturbing, chaotic, and frightening state of mind. To help him reach a comforting conclusion for his poem, I took an active role to provide resilience. I reminded him that he was the Candy King. He could change things. What would he do? The boy decided that he would tell the police to leave his chocolate land:

My chocolate land would be bad
There be bad people with 22s, machine guns,
shooting the chocolate police

But I'm the Candy King
I'd just tell the police to leave
my chocolate land

List Poem

The List Poem is a very plastic structure that, in fact, is used in conjunction with many of the writing forms below: lists of emotions, lists of memories, lists of questions. I separate out the List Poem, too, as its own form, because of its versatility that includes lists of the things I miss about home, lists of changes I need to make in my life, lists of things I've lost, lists of things I've learned.

When the opening poem of chapter 9, "The Doors of Emotion," was created, I was working with a young woman who had a difficult time expressing her feelings. She was also new to poetry. So I asked her to imagine the closed doors in her mind. We then opened those doors one by one:

The Doors of Emotion
by a young woman in juvenile detention, age 15

I'm opening up closed doors
Behind one door you find sadness
It's blue, it's boring, it's lonely, it makes you cry

Behind another door
You see happy people enjoying things they like
You hate them because they're enjoying things and you're not
So you slam the door and move on to the next one

The next door is terrifying
You see guns and drugs and people dying
. . .

Poetic-Imagery Poem

If a teen can articulate a feeling, a writing mentor can help her create a successful poem using poetic imagery. As described in previous chapters, the teen may need a series of examples to help her understand the structure of a simile or metaphor, and to start her own thinking. For example, if a teen is angry, a mentor might ask if she feels like a bomb ready to explode, or like a monster ripping up a city, or like cornered rat, or ???. (The three question marks are a Pongo cue, representing a mentor's openness to a teen's own creative ideas.) Here is an excerpt from a poem about loneliness, facilitated by a Pongo mentor:

Not Feeling Cared For
by a young woman in juvenile detention, age 16

I feel alone
Like a deer that's just been born
But its mom died
Like the only flower
In a field
Like a pool of water
In the middle of the desert

I feel deserted
Like an open piece of candy on the shelf
. . .
I feel the need for love
A squeeze of lemon in my glass of water
. . .

Emotion Poem

Many distressed teens have strong emotions. These can be the subject of relevant and powerful poems that effectively address feelings, reactions, and causes of a particular emotional state. A poem about anger can ask one or all of these questions:

What is it like to feel angry?

What happens to you when you're angry?

What are the causes of your anger?

The answer to each question might include detailed anecdotes or poetic imagery. In the excerpt below, the poem ends by repeating its first line, which raises an essential question within the poem—Why is it that the author's anger is a mystery to him?

My Anger Is a Mystery to Me
by a young man in juvenile detention, age 14

My anger is a mystery to me

Sometimes when I get angry
I don't realize it
I just go after people
I use drugs to calm me down
I just need to smoke a cigarette

Sometimes when I get angry
I feel like the world is out to get me
. . .

. . .
My anger is a mystery to me

Chronology/Memory Poem
The author is this example is a homeless teen. She had already written a great deal with me on other days and was short of ideas during this session. I asked her to proceed step-by-step through a series of memories—"I remember when I was five," "I remember when I was six," etc. The poem naturally captures a process in which her life went downhill. The last stanza (not included here) wraps up the poem by describing her life today. At fifteen years old, she feels "tired" and ready to make a change.

Early Memories
by a young woman in a center for homeless youth, age 15 . . .

I remember
I was 6
and everybody in my first-grade class
got the chicken pox.
For a month
there were no more than two kids in class.

I learned to block out
the itch with my mind.
I really got good at it,
and I still do it today.

. . .

I remember
when I was 10
things weren't going so good at home.
I got kicked out of school
because I never went
and because I beat up kids.
I stayed with friends
and partied
with their older brothers and sisters.

. . .

Sensory Poem

A mentor can help a teen to write about an event by structuring a poem based
on sensory experiences. In this example, I used a sensory form for teens in
a therapy group on traumatic grief. The group was in a juvenile rehabilitation facility, and all the group members had experienced the violent loss of
someone close to them. Each stanza in the form asks the author to describe a
different sensory experience associated with the traumatic death. I helped the
boy wrap up the poem by creating a last stanza about the way he feels today.
When this boy finished the poem below, his counselor said it was the most
she had heard him talk in a year:

When Death Comes Suddenly
by a young man in juvenile rehabilitation, age 13

. . .

The things I've heard.
Gunshots. It wasn't really loud because they were right in front of me.
More than 100 shots from automatic weapons. They shot the whole car up.
Plus my cousin got shot 15 times.

The things I've touched.
I held his hand. He lived for three hours when he got fixed up.
His hand was soft, clean.
And I had a flashback at the time. I could have died.

The things I've tasted.
We just finished eating at McDonald's.
We'd kicked it that day. Gone to the mall.
A bag of new clothes on the backseat got shot up.
There was cotton all over the place.
    . . .

What-If Poem

Many teens find themselves in dire circumstances. The structure of "What If" can be very relevant, or at least interesting, for a teen. It can provide an opportunity to reflect on effects and causality, for example. Here are several lines from one teen's poem:

What If Alcohol
by a young man in juvenile detention, age 17

If alcohol was never invented
People would remember what crimes they committed
    . . .
If alcohol was never invented
Children wouldn't grow up to be alcoholics
    . . .
If alcohol was never invented
I would never have to feel guilty or have regrets
    . . .

Here are some examples of "What If" questions that could be turned into poems:

What if you didn't have to be here now?

What if you woke up and this was all a dream?

What if alcohol was never invented?

What if there was no TV?

What if there was a community center on every corner, open 24/7?

What if people were loved as much as they should be?

What if mothers and fathers always listened to their kids?

What if kids ran their families?

What if you could have anything you wanted?

Repeated-Line Poem

Sometimes a teen may start to dictate her thoughts, then stall. A mentor might recognize resonance in one line already expressed. That strong line can become the basis for a new poem by repeating it as a refrain, and working with the teen to create lines or stanzas that will be followed by the repeated line. The new poem might have both thematic power and rhythm. Here is an excerpt from a poem that I facilitated with a homeless teen, in which the line "Whose fault was that" is repeated. The repeated line raises the important issue of guilt and responsibility in troubled families:

Whose Fault Was
by a young woman in a center for homeless youth, age 15(?)

. . .
We don't talk to each other enough
  Whose fault was that
But isn't she my mother
  Whose fault was that
She was never there for me
  Whose fault was that
She lied a lot in the past
  Whose fault was that
But I think she tries hard
  Whose fault was that
. . .

Good/Bad Poem

Many of Pongo's authors have topics to express that are also difficult to approach directly because of their power, depth, or complicated nature. A writing mentor can help a teen to write by giving her the emotional space to consider different sides of an issue, such as the good and the bad. For example, a teen might want to write about her mom, but feel stymied by conflicted feelings. Here is an excerpt of a poem that I facilitated with a young woman in the state psychiatric hospital, in which the form of good and bad helped her to include difficult feelings:

Good Experience/Bad Experience
by a young woman in the state psychiatric hospital, age 14

A good experience—I learned
not to lean back in chairs

. . .

A bad experience—With
hurting people

. . .

A good experience—Trying to learn
to dance

. . .

A bad experience—Hurting myself

. . .

Question Poem

Sometimes a teen is so conflicted and confused that it is difficult for him to write anything that expresses a concrete point of view. A writing mentor can facilitate an interesting poem by explaining that a person doesn't always need the answers in life. Sometimes it's important to articulate the questions. Here is an excerpt from a poem of questions:

Questions
by a young man in a center for LGBTQ youth, age 19

. . .

Why is the real world such a burden?
How will I ever be respected?

Why am I in so much pain?
Why did I never get in touch with my emotions?
. . .

Being Creative

The Pongo Method calls on a writing mentor to be a patient listener with distressed youth, and a kind facilitator of their personal poetry. In this process there are many opportunities for a mentor's creativity, in her choice of poems to share, in her own poetry in response to the work, and especially in her collaboration, in the moment, with a teen writer. The ten writing forms are one opportunity, though just a starting point, in that collaborative creative process.

12

Using Fill-in-the-Blank Activities

The Lessons of Courage and Fear
by a young woman, age 16

In my life I've known Courage.
We met when I had my baby boy.
Nowadays Courage is standing by my side.
I find Courage when I face my fear and speak my mind.

In my life I've known Fear.
We met when I got sexually abused.
These days Fear is the nightmares that don't let me sleep.
Fear finds me when I see those guys that have hurt me.

I've learned that Courage and Fear are different.
When Courage tells me that I am strong
and I don't have to look behind,
Fear says I'll never be me again.
Usually I listen to Courage, Fear, and my heart.
I wish no one may know my fears
and only see my courage and strength
so that I can be me again.
I wish I was Courage and not Fear.

The opening poem, "The Lessons of Courage and Fear," was written and submitted to Pongo using a fill-in-the-blank writing activity on the Pongo Teen Writing website. This is a moving and personal poem that was created by an inexperienced writer. It represents the particular benefit of *Using a Fill-in-the-Blank*, which is a third writing mode, in addition to *Taking Dictation* and *Improvising a Poetic Structure*.

The opportunity in *Using a Fill-in-the-Blank* is that it is based on a highly structured writing activity that expresses an emotionally relevant theme in a compelling poetic form. Even when a teen is hurt or stuck or withholding or inexperienced with poetry, she can often write easily and with great satisfaction using this framework, especially if she has the opportunity to work along with an adult mentor. There are two examples of fill-in-the-blank activities included in this chapter, "The Lessons of Courage and Fear" (figure 12.1, on which the opening poem is based) and "I Just Thought You Should Know" (figure 12.2).

In a one-on-one session, a mentor can turn to fill-in-the-blanks whenever a youth is having difficulty making a beginning, or whenever a youth is having difficulty reflecting insightfully on his own life and feelings. Fill-in-the-blanks are also very effective in groups and can be used as a writing warm-up or as the main writing activity in a classroom or therapy group.

To make these activities available to youth in a one-on-one session, Pongo uses activity binders with a table of contents, tabs, and multiple copies of twenty-five different activities. At the opportune time the mentor might grab the binder, show the table of contents to the teen, make activity suggestions, and encourage the individual to browse the different options. When a youth chooses an activity to complete, he may prefer to complete it on his own, but he may also appreciate having the mentor's help. In that case, the mentor might read the example poem to the youth and then read the activity aloud, line by line, while taking down the teen's responses and offering ideas as necessary to keep the process flowing.

When the mentor is assisting the youth with a fill-in-the-blank, he would follow the techniques of *Taking Dictation*, including praising the teen's work, reading back the teen's work periodically in the process, making suggestions for content (such as requesting elaborations of feelings and sensory experiences), and being flexible in terms of allowing the teen ultimate control. In each activity the teen writer is always encouraged to cross out or alter lines, or make any creative changes he wants on the fill-in-the-blank forms.

Pongo has fifty of these fill-in-the-blank activities available on our website, and each activity can be completed by a youth online and also downloaded as a Word file for teachers and counselors to print out and use with an individual or group. Most of the activities follow the form of those provided here: Most are two pages long with an example poem on the first page and the fill-in-the-blank exercise, including possible responses, on the second page.

Name:

Date:

THE LESSONS OF COURAGE AND FEAR

The purpose of this writing activity is to describe some of your experiences with courage and fear in a poem. Read the example below and then complete the writing exercise that follows.

THE LESSONS OF COURAGE AND FEAR
by Kate

In my life I've known Courage.
We met when I was six, fending off a shadowy figure
in a scary dream.
Nowadays Courage comforts me every time I confront shadows
no one else seems to see.

In my life I've known Fear.
We met when I heard the sound of my dad's voice
raised in anger.
These days Fear tricks me with Worry every time I'm in a position
to harm or be harmed.

I've learned that Courage and Fear are similar—
They both influence my course of action.
I've also learned they're different—
When Courage tells me, "Leave it be,"
Fear says, "Beware!" and, "Prepare for a fight."
Usually I listen to Fear.
I wish Courage could talk directly to Fear
and leave me out of the loop.

FIGURE 12.1
"The Lessons of Courage and Fear" Writing Activity

Fill in the blanks in the poem below. Use the words suggested or choose your own words to communicate your thoughts as clearly and powerfully as you can. Feel free to add lines, remove lines, or change words to fit your purpose.

THE LESSONS OF COURAGE AND FEAR

In my life I've known Courage.
We met when I _____.
> *(first stepped between my mom and dad fighting,*
> *was seven and taking care of my brother alone, ???)*

Nowadays Courage is _____.
> *(walking ahead of me, abandoning me, ???).*

I find Courage when _____.
> *(I'm out on the streets, I'm sitting before the judge, ???)*

In my life I've known Fear.
We met when I _____.
> *(took my first hit, was six and left alone at home, ???)*

These days Fear is _____.
> *(sending my heart racing, creeping up behind me, ???)*

Fear finds me when _____.
> *(someone tells me I've done something wrong,*
> *my mom flies into a rage, ???)*

I've learned that Courage and Fear are different—
When Courage tells me _____,
> *(to leave my friends behind, Don't back down!, ???)*

Fear says _____.
> *(be the first to throw the punch,*
> *you'll never make it on your own, ???)*

Usually I listen to _____.
> *(Courage, Fear, my gut, ???)*

I wish _____.
> *(my Courage didn't look so much like Fear,*
> *I could get others to listen to my Fear, ???)*

I wish _____.

FIGURE 12.1
(*continued*)

Name:

Date:

I JUST THOUGHT YOU SHOULD KNOW

The purpose of this exercise is to communicate your thoughts and feelings to a person you may not see much anymore, due to life circumstances. This is a chance to say things you never had a chance to say, or to tell this important person about yourself—the challenges you have faced, the achievements you have accomplished, and how these things have made you who you are today.

Read the poem below, and then complete the writing exercise on the next page.

A LETTER TO MY DAD
by Sam (age 15)

I just thought you should know what I'm doing now.
I am a strong person who spends his time
looking for ways to become more successful.

I just thought you should know how I'm feeling.
I am pissed because you couldn't be here and watch me grow.
It puts tears in my eyes knowing my father wasn't there.

I just thought you should know what I've been through
without seeing you. Since the last time I saw you I have
grown so much it would blow you away.

The moment I knew I could survive without you is important to me.

What I don't miss is you and your old life. At least
you don't have to worry about your son going down that path.

I just thought you should know
that I wish you could see my success.

FIGURE 12.2
"I Just Thought You Should Know" Writing Activity

I JUST THOUGHT YOU SHOULD KNOW *(continued)*

Fill in the blanks in the poem below. Use the words suggested or choose your own words to communicate your thoughts as clearly and powerfully as you can. Feel free to add lines of your own, to remove lines, or to change words to fit your purpose.

Dear _____ *(Mom, Dad, Sister, Grandma, old friend, ???)*,

I just thought you should know what I'm doing now.
    I am a _____ *(strong, angry, happy, lonely, ???)* person
    who spends a lot of time _____
    (dancing, watching movies, hanging out with my friends, ???).

I just thought you should know how I'm feeling.
    I am _____ *(happy, nervous, depressed, ???)*
    because _____.

I just thought you should know what I've been through.
    Since the last time I saw you, I have _____
    (grown, suffered, changed, ???) so much. The time that I _____
    _____ was especially important.

I just thought you should know what I wish for the future.
    I hope that _____
    _____.

I just thought you should know what I don't miss about you.
    I am glad I don't have to worry about _____
    _____ anymore.

I just thought you should know what I miss a lot.
    I miss the way *(you, we)* used to _____
    _____.

I just thought you should know _____.

FIGURE 12.2
(continued)

13

Overview of the Group Process

Who Am I?
by a young woman in juvenile detention, age 14

When I was born I thought I'd be an innocent child
But now I'm here in juvenile
Like my mother, out running the streets
Smoking crack and robbing people for money
And I thought, Who Am I?
I lost my virginity to a guy I didn't know
Hanging out with older people
Who just wanted to get in my pants
Thinking I could get in the game
And I thought, Who Am I?
It's harsh out there
All you do is sit waiting for crack
Spending your money on crack
Being a crack whore
And I thought, Who Am I?
People running in and out
Worrying about cops
Being thrown in the back of a police car

And thinking, Who Am I?
And now I sit in my room
Thinking about what to do with my life
Be like my mother, or be like myself
I'm ending up like her
But I'm different
I can change my ways
And I'm not like anybody else
And I thought to myself
That is Who I Am

Dedicated to my friend and loving mother

In the Pongo Method, everything that happens during a successful group writing session contributes to a happy, supportive, and transformative *group culture*, whose heart is the writers' enthusiasm for their own personal writing and their support for the personal writing of their peers. In such a group, the youth express the group's values at the beginning of the writing session each week and bring newcomers on board to those values. In such a group, the youth become the leaders. They express what they want and need. In such a group, the youth guide the adults.

Establishing this group culture can be a peak experience of the work. In a group like this, the youth will grow up together, and grow up more quickly, more naturally, and with more fun than an adult alone can effect. When a successful group is made up of youth who in their previous lives have suffered greatly, the rapid emotional progress of the group members feels miraculous.

Of course, the pace of change within the group will vary depending on whether there is a stable group of participants each week. However, even when a mentor works with different youth each week, her purposes and goodness can be established broadly within the community of an institution or agency, as someone who consistently provides a warm, satisfying, creative experience for youth.

This chapter will describe two models of group, a "Classic" Pongo model and a "Classroom" Pongo model. These models are *starting points*, frameworks within which a writing mentor can experiment, to make a successful experience for the youth in her care. The end of this chapter includes suggestions about the makeup of groups. It also offers suggestions of sources for group writing activities.

Two Types of Writing Groups

So far this book has focused on Pongo's "Classic" model in which mentors and youth work one-on-one in the same room, which includes a purposeful introduction to the experience, perhaps a full-group warm-up writing activity at the beginning of the hour, and a poetry sharing circle to end the experience.

Alternatively, a mentor may be working with youth in what is described below as the "Classroom" Pongo model. A mentor may be a teacher with a class, or a therapist with a group. In this situation the mentor may be one adult with a group of youth. She would still be guided by the Pongo approach and intentions, but she would need to facilitate a group experience that includes successful, *independent* personal writing by the youth, without the benefit of one-on-one mentorship.

This chapter will describe these two specific models of groups, "Classic" and "Classroom." The models are structured as follows:

The "Classic" Pongo Model includes

- Introduction
- Group writing activity as warm-up
- One-on-one writing by youth with mentors
- Group sharing at end

The "Classroom" Pongo Model includes

- Introduction
- Group writing activity with relevant theme
- Independent writing by youth on theme (following the theme that was previously introduced)
- Group sharing at end

In the descriptions of these group models, I will sometimes refer to the contributions of Ann Teplick and Robin Brownstein. Ann is a writer and writing teacher who joined Pongo twelve years ago, in Pongo's first group of volunteers. Ann led the Pongo project in juvenile detention for three years and has now led the Pongo project in the state psychiatric hospital for children for seven years. Robin is a clinical social worker who, after receiving training and coaching from Pongo, formed the first Pongo "duckling" project, an independent writing project that follows the Pongo model. Robin has been leading Pongo duckling projects for four years.

"Classic" Pongo Writing Group

In the "Classic" Pongo Writing Group there are four parts to the writing session: Introduction, Writing Warm-Up, One-on-One Writing by Youth with Mentors, and Group Sharing at End.

Pongo focuses on one-on-one work within our regular programs because the writing mentors work with an ever-shifting population of deeply suffering youth. The mentors often see our writers only once. In the one-on-one experience with these teens, the mentors have a unique opportunity to help the youth write in a profoundly personal and healing way, in a process that can teach the youth tools for life. Here are some specific guidelines for running the "Classic" group.

Introduction (5–10 minutes)

The introduction at the beginning of a group is the opportunity to welcome people, state Pongo's purposes (as explained in chapter 8), share meaningful poetry, develop or share rules, and talk about what will happen in the writing session to come.

In her introduction to the group, the Pongo leader might vary the content to emphasize particular qualities of the experience, such as writing process (Ann, the writer) or therapeutic experience (Robin, the therapist). Here is a sample script for an introduction:

"Welcome. We are happy to see all of you today. Who has written poetry with Pongo before? Will you tell the others what it's like? Who has written poetry before but not with Pongo? Did any of you bring poetry with you today? Good. Let's hear a couple of your poems.

"Let me tell you a few things about Pongo and poetry. We've been working with teens at sites like this one for seventeen years. We ask that people 'Write from the heart about who you are.' We believe that 'Honesty is the most important quality of good poetry.' We believe that 'People who have had difficult experiences have important things to share with the world.'

"Pongo has published books of teen writing, and we have a website, and we may be able to include some poems from this year in our next book, though we can't promise.

"Today we'll talk about poetry, then you'll have a chance to work one-on-one with a mentor who can help you write, even if it's your first time writing. At the end we'll gather together, and you'll have a chance to share your writing, if you want."

In addition to this script, the group introduction will likely include mention of at least some of the following four topics, which are covered in more detail in the discussion of safety in chapter 7. These topics are overlapping (e.g., "safety" can include the others, as can "rules").

- *Safety*: A group leader needs to demonstrate an awareness and ability to maintain a safe group. Pongo leader Ann's introduction to her writing group at the psychiatric hospital includes the statement "We strive to make this a safe space." She will then ask the youth to express what safety means to them. See the next chapter for more suggestions on running a safe group.
- *Rules*: The group rules can be developed initially by the youth and then restated week to week. The rules will include mutual respect and will support safety. Pongo leader Robin's rules are the following: "(1) We write from the heart, (2) This is a safe space [No judgment. No criticism. What we bring into this space stays here.], and (3) You can write here about whatever you want."
- *Confidentiality*: The essence of confidentiality is that the teens' privacy will be maintained outside the agency and institution. For example, Pongo uses pseudonyms when we publish youth poetry. Also, as a necessity for youth comfort and safety, another aspect of confidentiality is that a young person's poetry should not be shared with other youth without the author's consent. In addition, therefore, confidentiality includes an understanding

among the youth in a group that they will respect one another's privacy after they leave the group. In her work, therapist Robin uses a discussion of confidentiality as a support to encourage openness in her writing group.

- *Reporting*: There are legal and ethical requirements for adults to report situations in which a young person is at imminent risk of being hurt. This reporting requirement is best disclosed to a group at the beginning of a session. A mentor's concerns about a particular teen are most easily discussed with a youth at the end of the session. To inform youth about reporting requirements, Pongo will sometimes show youth a card that has a brief statement on this topic, as explained in chapter 7.

In addition to the parts of the introduction already described (script and safety discussion), the adult leader will share poetry on topics that are meaningful for the youth. The leader might hand out copies of these poems and say, "Now, let's look at some poetry that other teens have written on some important topics. You'll see that poetry can speak to all kinds of complicated issues. Will you help me read these poems aloud? I'd like to hear what you think."

At this point, after representations of values, safety, and poetic emotion, the youth should feel inspired to write openly about their lives and feelings.

Group Writing Activity as Warm-Up (15–20 minutes)

When time is limited, for example in a session of 50 minutes or less, Pongo will eliminate the writing warm-up to preserve a full 30+ minutes for the one-on-one writing. However, when there is time, such as in a 90-minute writing period, a 15–20-minute group writing warm-up can bring the group together, increase dialogue, and stimulate creativity in preparation for the one-on-one.

The writing warm-up may take different forms. It may be an activity that people contribute to verbally, while the lead mentor records individual contributions on a whiteboard or easel. It may be a short, open-ended written activity, perhaps requiring one to three sentences, that participants write down on a blank piece of paper. It may be a handout, such as a Pongo fill-in-the-blank poem.

The mentors sit at the table and participate along with the youth in these writing warm-ups, and they assist the individual youth around them, as necessary.

For her writing warm-ups, Ann chooses a theme (e.g., love, heartbreak, family, alienation, hopes, dreams) for the day. She brings in a short poem on the theme and invites the youth to help her read aloud. The group discusses the poem, perhaps highlighting such poetic elements as imagery and repetition. Ann then provides a writing prompt, which she asks the youth to respond to in only three minutes, in a stream-of-consciousness way, without editing. Later, Ann collects the youth responses and types them up as a group poem. Some of Ann's prompts are as follows:

- To understand me, you need to know . . .
- These are the things that irk me . . .
- This is how to be brave . . .
- This is what stresses me . . .
- This is how I calm myself down . . .
- If I could change the world, I would . . .

Ann then goes around the room asking everyone to share, but she will give youth the option to be skipped. Usually after others have shared, the people who elected to be skipped will then decide to read their work or have it read by another.

Robin often incorporates an interpersonal "icebreaker" activity into her warm-up time, during which people might share their names and a creative piece of information about themselves.

One-on-One Writing by Youth with Mentors (30–45 minutes)

At this point in the "Classic" Pongo writing session, there is the opportunity for one-on-one writing. This writing follows the process and techniques that are described in chapters 9–12, in which the mentors and youth are paired up and spread out around the room. To ease the process of actually pairing a youth with a mentor, the Pongo leader will either assign youth to mentors arbitrarily or have the youth choose mentors by lot, from folded slips of paper.

Sitting with a youth, the mentor then guides the process, choosing a method of either *Taking Dictation, Improvising a Writing Structure, Using a Fill-in-the-Blank* activity, or possibly working independently, depending on the writer's need for support in the creative flow. If the mentor takes dictation, she may use a computer, if available, or a pad and pencil. The advantage of a computer is that the youth poetry does not need to be retyped later. Also, it is easier for a youth to review and edit her work by reading it on the mentor's computer. We do *not* allow the youth to work on their own on a computer because of the difficulties of damage (where some youth will change settings on computers) and distraction (where some youth will preoccupy themselves with formatting instead of writing).

Group Sharing at End (10–20 minutes)

Toward the end of the writing session, the Pongo leader will bring the youth and mentors together to share the youth writing. Some teens may be shy about sharing at first, but many can be encouraged to share, especially after others have led the way. Many youth would like to have their poems read, but are more comfortable if the mentor or another youth is the one to read their poetry aloud. This is an option that the leader always offers.

(When it is time to share, my own preference is to see if any youth will volunteer to read first, to get the ball rolling, before I invite others to read their work. After some youth have read, I will call on others, with an effort to be both encouraging and understanding of individuals who are shy. Often, if a person is hesitant to share, I will invite her to think about it, while I move on to someone else. Then I can check in with her again. I have another technique I like to use to increase participation: If a teen doesn't want to share her writing with the group, I invite her to share a single stanza or a single line.)

Some youth will have written multiple poems. It's best to limit every youth to reading just one poem, to give opportunities to everyone, before going around the room again to hear the rest of the poetry.

There may be rare instances when a Pongo leader decides, with the help of other mentors, that a poem is inappropriate and should not be shared with the group. A poem that is explicit and/or manipulative in its use of violent and sexual material may fall into this category.

Of course the teen writing that is shared will often be beautiful and painful and revealing and sad. It might represent a breakthrough in self-awareness for the writer. It might provoke tears but also be a great source of pride and relief for the writer. This time at the end of a session, when the youth and the writing mentors hear the teens' poetry, might be very moving for everyone. The mentors' special role is to listen, appreciate, and celebrate the youth as poets, as discussed in chapter 3.

"Classroom" Pongo Writing Group

In the "Classroom" Pongo Writing Group there are four parts to the writing session: Introduction, Group Writing Activity on a Relevant Theme, Independent Writing by Youth on Theme (following the theme that was previously introduced), and Group Sharing at End.

In the circumstances of working with a group, where there is not the opportunity for one-on-one writing, and where the group may be strangers to the writing mentor, the Pongo Method recommends that a mentor create a single relevant theme among (1) the poetry that is shared in the introduction, (2) the group writing activity, and (3) the individual writing exercise that follows. The Pongo Method also recommends that a mentor makes the group writing activity a verbal activity, in which teens can participate with ease, at their own comfort level, and through which a lot of ideas may be generated. The group writing activity and the individual exercise may even use the same writing activity.

Introduction (15 minutes)

The introduction (with welcome, statements of purpose, rules, and sample poetry, etc.) is the same as that in the "Classic" Pongo Writing Group, with the exception that the Pongo Method recommends that the writing mentor selects sample poetry that fits the theme of the group activity and individual writing to come. For example, if a mentor chooses a group writing activity such as "Home to Me" (figure 13.1) which was created by Ann and is included in this chapter, Pongo recommends that she also share sample poetry on the theme of "Home" during the introduction.

In this example, the poetry about home should represent complexity, covering the good and bad aspects of home, such as the warm and comforting, and also the disappointing and confusing possibilities that many teens experience. These are poems that a mentor would find in anthologies, or perhaps from among the youth poems on the Pongo website. As an example, for the theme of "Home," there is the poem "Missing My Family," which was taken from the Pongo website. Its subject is more about family than home, but it includes several memorable sensory images that would further a youth discussion of "Home."

Missing My Family
by a young woman in juvenile detention, age 14

Today is a typical day: boring, and going to school.
But a couple things are different.
I'm in a place of solitude, away from everyone,
and silent, as usual.
A lot of new people, a lot of new faces.
But there are a few that I miss the most.
My family.

We're a little chaotic, and tend to go insane sometimes.
If someone were to see us, they'd see us as disoriented.
It's kind of like when you shake a snow globe,
there's always a little clump of snow,
that sticks to the side of the glass and doesn't move—
that's my family.
But that's what makes us family.

My family are some of the loudest people on our block.
The neighbors hear us screaming about silly things,
like an old doll getting stuck in a tree.
It's been stuck there for like 4 or 5 years now,
even through the Washington wind storms.

My family has communication issues sometimes,
but we always have each other's back,
and we will never let each other down.

The saying in our family is: "You don't have to like the person,
but you do have to love them. They're family."

As in the "Classic" Writing Group model, above, a mentor could involve
the youth by supplying these poems as handouts, and then asking for volunteers from among the youth to read the poem samples aloud. The mentor

could then lead a discussion about each poem, what people liked and what they didn't like, what images and themes in the poems spoke to them.

Group Writing Activity on a Relevant Theme (15–30 minutes)

To involve the most teens, and to supply the greatest flow of ideas that can be translated into individual poems, the Pongo Method recommends that a mentor brings a group activity to which the youth can contribute verbally. The lead writing mentor creates a poem during the discussion by recording the teens' ideas on a whiteboard or easel. The youth can participate as they feel comfortable, with less inhibition, and with the opportunity to be stimulated by one another and to interact with one another.

As an example, the writing mentor could recreate the "Home to Me" activity on a whiteboard or easel, and invite contributions from many youth in each category. (Please refer to the "Home to Me" fill-in-the-blank activity, in this chapter.) In this case, the first group discussion would be to complete this sentence: "When I think of home I SEE . . . . " The teens' different ideas would then be listed.

As the mentor collects ideas for sights of home in this example, she can offer lots of creative suggestions to further stimulate the discussion, suggesting that youth describe objects in their rooms and special people in their lives. The mentor can ask the youth to elaborate on their ideas, so that "stuffed animal" becomes "the stuffed green frog my dad gave me on my birthday." The mentor can sensitively invite good and bad experiences, so that "my sister's loving smile" might be complemented by "and my brother's angry scowl." She can teach simile and metaphor. What is "Home" like—a nest of chicks, a school of piranha, or ???. As the activity progresses, the mentor would read this group poem aloud periodically, to reinforce what the youth have accomplished.

This "Home" activity moves through sights, sounds, smells, and tastes of home. After the mentor progresses through the various sensory experiences of home, she can end by inviting a discussion of the teens' feelings about home.

Again, the advantage of this verbal process is that youth can participate comfortably, while they are exposed to lots of ideas, and can interact positively with writing mentors and with other youth. In this process the mentor will have many opportunities to connect with youth who are shy and quiet. She can ask for ideas and input from quiet youth, without pressure, and then praise every effort they make to contribute.

Independent Writing on a Theme (15–30 minutes)

As a follow-up to the group poem, the participants are handed a structured writing activity (e.g., a fill-in-the-blank poem) on the same theme, perhaps the very same activity that they worked on as a group, to complete by working independently. At this stage the writing mentor and her colleagues can circulate around the room to help the youth. At this point, after exposure to ideas and expectations, most of the youth should find the activity easy to complete.

In the "Home to Me" example, a mentor might distribute printouts of the activity for the youth to complete on their own. It's certainly possible that the youth in the group would be able to write on a more general and less structured assignment than a fill-in-the-blank. In addition, the Pongo Method always gives the youth the option of writing a wholly unique, personal poem when they are working on their own, rather than require that everyone complete the structured activity that serves some youth so well.

In the end, the writing mentor will probably be surprised at the original and personal issues that the youth express in their writing while working on their own, because they have been given the advantages of (1) a writing structure, (2) lots of ideas, and (3) an important theme.

Group Sharing at End (15 minutes)

The group sharing at the end of the activity is the same as the group sharing described above for the "Classic" Pongo writing group, except that the writing mentor will need to allow more time to accommodate a larger "Classroom" group.

Other Planning and Considerations for a Group

Here are some of the planning and other considerations for a group:

1. *Age makeup of group*: In general, youth in their teens are more concrete in wanting to write about their lives, while preteens are often happier in fantasy writing. The personal issues of teenagers may be inappropriate for

preteens. Pongo recommends that mentors not mix teens and preteens in a writing group.

2. *Gender makeup of group:* Robin's first writing group evolved into a girls' group with a core cohort of participants over several years. There was great power for the members in supporting one another's growth through a girls-only writing group.

3. *Supplies:* A mentor will need pads and pens and, if possible, computers. A mentor will need handouts of poems and writing activities. In addition, a mentor may need a portable easel, big pad, and marking pens.

4. *Food:* Providing food at the beginning can be a positive lure and support for a writing group. It is not possible in many settings, such as institutions.

Other planning issues are discussed elsewhere in this book. For example, the issues of typing and saving teens' work (and more) are described in chapter 6, and the issues of publishing and Writer Release forms are described in chapter 15.

Finding and Creating a Group Activity

Writing mentors who are new to teaching writing will find that they become collectors, creators, and connoisseurs of group writing activities. Over time, writing mentors will hunt for activities, modify them, make new activities, and save effective activities in valued collections to use in the future. As a start, here are some ideas for finding and creating group writing activities:

- Pongo has fifty fill-in-the-blank writing activities on its website (www.pongoteenwriting.org). Each activity can be downloaded by a writing mentor as a Word file, to later print and hand out to a group. Many of these activities can be used for a verbal group activity, or at least can inspire a related verbal group activity.

- Pongo suggests ten concepts for improvised poetic structures, as described in chapter 11. These suggestions include wishes, lists, emotions, memories, senses, what-if propositions, good/bad considerations, and questions. Each of these concepts can be the foundation for any number of successful and relevant group activities for distressed youth.

- In chapter 10, in the description of *Taking Dictation*, there is a discussion of including sources of resilience as part of a poem. Sources of resilience, including values, personal qualities, supportive people in a poet's life, and founts of strength can all provide great topics for writing activities.
- By reading lots of poetry, in particular poetry on emotional themes, a mentor will find examples that will inspire distressed youth. Among these examples there will be poems that have a resonant line or simple structure that can be adapted to create a fill-in-the-blank for another group activity. The Pongo website has a list of poetry anthologies on emotional themes.
- In books and on the Internet a mentor can find teacher resources that include writing activities. Many of these activities will be based on poetic forms (e.g., a haiku) or will utilize enjoyable ways of engaging youth (e.g., using physical objects for inspiration). These can be very useful, especially if a mentor adapts these activities to include themes that speak to the emotional concerns of distressed youth.
- And, of course, a mentor may want to create her own poetry that can be adapted to form the basis of a group writing activity.

Name:

Date:

HOME TO ME

The purpose of this activity is to think and write about the theme of "home" and what home means to us, both good and bad. Please read the poem below, and then go to the next page to create a poem of your own.

HOME TO ME
by Ann

Barley soup thick with sweet onions
Chipped dishes, mismatched china
Stuffing tumbled from easy chairs
Yellow curtains, gauzy with wind
Jazz on the FM, trumpet and drums
Mom in the bathtub, bubbled in strawberry
Dad kneading bread
House full of tabbies, hair on the pillow
Sirens at midnight, three a.m., five
Shouting from the apartment above
Radiator rusted, north windows cracked
Burnt mac and cheese, orange as sunrise
Warm and secure
Family of love.

Activity Copyright © 2007 Ann Teplick

FIGURE 13.1
"Home to Me" Writing Activity

HOME TO ME *(continued)*

Please fill in the blanks of the poem below. Focus on details. Feel free to add or remove words or lines to make this poem one that has meaning for YOU.

When I think of my home I SEE_____.
(my brother playing baseball in the grassy lot next door,
mold on the pea-green bathroom wall, ???)

When I think of my home I HEAR_____.
(shouting and glass breaking in the neighborhood,
Grandma singing the blues, ???)

When I think of home I SMELL_____.
(buttermilk pancakes on Saturday morning,
garbage from the metal can next door, ???)

When I think of home I TASTE_____.
(fuzz on my tongue first thing in the morning,
my sister's peppermint toothpaste, ???)

When I think of home I TOUCH _____.
(my flannel sheets in a frosty January,
the scratchy fur of my terrier Bob, ???)

When I think of my home I FEEL _____.
(safe because I have a family who loves and protects me,
sad because no one takes the time to talk to me, ???)

When I think of my home I FEEL _____
_____.

FIGURE 13.1
(*continued*)

14

The Challenges of Group Process

Nuttcase
by young man in a center for homeless youth, age 16

As I sit here I think about my life
being disgusted.
Often people tell me that with them
I can't be trusted.
So now I reminisce about
the times I used to have.
Always the good things to
cheer me up and make me laugh.
But now my mind is
blurry, most of it hazy.
Sometimes I sit and think,
am I that damn crazy?
I get mad nowadays thinkin'
about the drugs that I used.
Then I think I'm a walkin'
time bomb with a short-ass fuse.

The process during a group writing activity can be one of the most reward-ing parts of a writing project. But there are particular challenges to this work, especially if the youth are strangers to the writing mentor, especially if the youth are meeting with the mentor within an institution or agency, and most especially if the youth are writing with the mentor involuntarily.

In the "Classic" Pongo Model of a project, the youth are working with Pongo voluntarily (though Pongo is constantly encouraging and prioritizing new writers). However, a mentor may find that he wants or needs to present a writing activity to a group in which every youth is required to participate.

The burdens can be great for distressed youth who are required to participate in a writing group. They may be frightened and resistant. We know that teens who are in distress from childhood abuse and neglect, or other trauma, may have a level of confusion that is a barrier to understanding. There is a part of them that may not want to be open to their experiences and feelings. In addition, these youth may feel terrible about themselves and may feel vulnerable to criticism and failure. With all of the distractions of their difficult life experiences, and perhaps for other reasons as well, the youth may never have enjoyed success in school or in using language skills before. Finally, these youth may be reluctant to trust others, with good historical reason.

In a one-on-one session, Pongo is able to address these challenges through the supportive writer-mentor relationship. But for teens in a group, the levels of confusion, vulnerability, and risk of being hurt are greater, and the opportunities for an adult to offer support are less direct.

Ultimately, with a group, the most significant new challenge for a writing mentor is the need to manage group dynamics, the ways in which the youth interact (or don't interact) with the *mentor and one another*. This chapter will discuss some of the difficult dynamics within groups, discuss how to manage a group, and provide some general advice on preparing for and leading a group.

Interpersonal Dynamics within a Group

When working with teens whose levels of confusion, vulnerability, and resistance are greater, the writing mentor must apply the Pongo Method assiduously to help the teens feel purposeful and safe in personal expression. Even then, there are particular challenges in group dynamics.

Teens in the aftermath of childhood trauma may engage in behavior within a group that may be subtle, disruptive, and even destructive. For example, a bully may intimidate a group and make other youth afraid to participate. Some youth in the group may ally themselves with the bully as a way of protecting themselves. The bully may then undermine the group by encouraging an ally to provoke a third individual, the victim. Of course, it is the victim who eventually explodes in anger and gets into trouble. Sometimes the bully's ally also gets in trouble. More rarely, the bully gets in trouble. A situation like this can be hard to follow as it is happening. For the writing mentor, one way of possibly turning this situation around is to engage the bully as a group leader and source of creative ideas.

Another challenge to groups is that teens may have needs and behaviors that are difficult to understand, and are more difficult to respond to in a group situation. For example, once at the psychiatric hospital, a girl was reading her poem at a microphone. Aware that the group was having trouble hearing the girl, I approached her to adjust the microphone, and she raised her hand to the side of her face as if to protect herself from a blow. I made a mental note not to approach students unexpectedly in the future.

Another challenge of working with youth in groups is that some individuals have problems that cause them to turn authority figures into "bad guys," to a greater degree even than the normal issues of adolescence. I remember a girl at a homeless shelter who was confrontational in this way. I can only imagine the chaos in the girl's life on the streets that added to her difficulty in ceding any control to me. A mentor can find himself confused by the resistance to his intentions, only to find that the more he tries to adapt, the more he is resisted. One possible way to rescue this situation is to give the disruptive individual an independent opportunity to write and express herself on topics of importance to her.

There is the challenge of youth who try to show off or say things for effect, in a group context, to impress or amuse their peers. For example, a teen may talk about drugs in a boastful way, as a joke, to get attention and laughter from peers. One possible way for a mentor to respond is to calmly recognize what is going on, without taking offense, and to redirect the conversation. Another possible way to respond is to recognize the seriousness of drugs for many people in pain, and invite a dialogue.

There is the challenge in which youth might be upset, angry, and distracted by events outside the writing group, such as a gang murder in the community or a fight inside the institution. One possible response is to allow an opportunity for discussion and writing, if it can be done safely (e.g., without provoking gang animosities or impulsive behavior).

Finally, there is the challenge of engaging youth who may be fearful, quiet, and shy. Although this is not "acting out" behavior *per se*, the mentor's task is to find a way for even the most isolated member to experience inclusion. *The most constant challenge for a writing mentor is to interact with and engage all the group members.*

These types of challenges are ameliorated once the writing group is established and it becomes a trusted source of expression and validation for the teens. These types of challenges are also ameliorated when the writing mentor has more experience with teens' particular vulnerabilities and behaviors, and can adapt to them in a nonconfrontational, effective way.

Managing a Group

In Pongo's experience, adolescents have significant vulnerabilities that are also understandable and rational. A writing mentor can avoid many of the teens' acting-out or isolative behaviors if he recognizes and responds to the following needs of teens:

1. They want respect.
2. They often believe the worst about a mentor's attitudes toward them.
3. They often believe the worst about their own ability to succeed.
4. They are extremely sensitive.
5. They are very concerned about being shamed in front of others, perhaps most particularly their peers.
6. They often feel controlled and powerless.
7. They are self-conscious about their history, and they want privacy.
8. They are worried about how safe a mentor is, and if the mentor is able to control the class.
9. They may be worried about how safe their fellow students will be.
10. They may need help controlling their impulses.

Table 14.1 lists some attitudes that a mentor can hold, some things he can do, and some words he can say, in order to interact with youth in groups in the most positive way.

Table 14.1. Key Messages for Groups

Key Messages/Plans for Groups	Words That Support Messages
Be high on expectations of youth.	Words: "You have important things to say and can say them really well."
Be low key about possible results.	Words: "Writing can be difficult for anyone, and it can be hard to express or listen to difficult feelings. Just do your best here."
Involve the youth in setting expectations and rules.	Words: "How would you like the group to go today? How would you like people to behave toward one another?"
Listen and give people a sense of control, where it isn't disruptive or distracting.	Words: "You said you are having a hard time reading my handwriting? Thanks for letting me know. I will try to write more clearly."
Try to engage people who may be afraid, shy, or quiet—recognizing that it may take a few tries (or a few sessions) to engage them, even if you are being sensitive, gentle, and encouraging.	Words: "Dustin, I'm interested in your ideas. Do you have anything to add to what the others have said?"
If a young person is a leader in disrupting a group, try to engage that person as a leader of the group process.	Words: "I have a poem I want to share with the group. Would you read it aloud for me?"
In guiding the group, speak from the perspective of higher principles.	Words: "You'll have to excuse me if I don't let you read a second poem, right now. I think the fairest thing is to give everyone a chance to read one poem first."
If a young person's behavior seems to be wrong, a mentor should recognize his own feelings of discomfort in the situation, trust his instincts, and not simply go on without reacting.	Words: "I don't know exactly what is happening between the two of you right now, but I'm concerned that it will distract from the writing activity, so I am asking you to…"

(*continued*)

Table 14.1. (*continued*)

Key Messages/Plans for Groups	Words That Support Messages
When a problem arises, be high on hopes for resolution.	Words: "I would really like it if we can work this out so you can be here."
Provide opportunities for youth to offer solutions to a problem.	Words: "What would you like to do to improve this situation, or what would you like me to do?"
Articulate concerns clearly and without blame.	Words: "I'm not comfortable with what is happening right now because people seem to be getting angry, so let's change our focus."
Always approach a problem situation with a neutral tone and without making snap judgments about individuals.	Words: "This is what needs to happen next…"
Whenever possible *assert limits on behavior with humility, humor, appreciation, and distraction.*	Words: "I may be wrong in my assessment of this situation, but…" or "I like your sense of humor, however…" or "On a different note, let's…"
Recognize that some situations will require a mentor to assert adult responsibility, particularly on issues of intimidation and safety.	Words: "It's inappropriate in here to joke about violence toward others."
Ask for advice from colleagues or institutional authorities at any time.	Words: "Mr. Smith, can you give us advice in this situation? Does the institution have a policy about this?"
Recognize that rare situations will require a mentor to exclude an individual from a group, end a group, or find a new agency in which to hold a writing group.	
Have backup plans, alternative activities, and strategies with colleagues in case plans must be changed during group.	
Understand that, ultimately, the youth are looking to a mentor to be strong—strong enough to care, strong enough to hear their pain, strong enough to keep them safe, and strong enough to be a feeling person.	

Preparing For and Leading a Group

It is necessary to prepare for and adapt to a wide variety of populations and changing or surprising circumstances. A mentor might go into a group expecting fifteen writers, and have forty walk in. He might go into a group expecting fifteen writers, and have four walk in. A mentor might find that his group is severely emotionally disturbed, perhaps heavily medicated, and capable of only limited emotional response. He might find that his group has only three over-stimulated middle-school writers, and includes a boy who is completed infatuated with the lone girl in the group, and completely incapable of attending to anything else. He might find that there was a fight in the institution beforehand, someone was injured, and the youth can think and talk about nothing else. He might find that in his early December writing group, with the holidays fast approaching, the entire group is deeply depressed.

A mentor might find, after he arrives at an institution, that key staff weren't informed he would be there, and they are resentful and uncooperative. He might find that he has been assigned to an airless room that is unbearably hot and stuffy. He might find, only after he arrives, that the youth are all on an outing or the staff is all at a meeting, and the writing session has to be canceled. A mentor might find that different staff are interpreting rules differently on a particular day, and, unexpectedly, he is no longer allowed to bring in stapled materials as handouts. He might find that the records that give him permission to enter the institution are suddenly unavailable because a computer is down.

It is in this context, of working with an unknown and vulnerable population, in a setting that is highly controlled but very much out of his control, that a writing mentor has to be materially and mentally prepared as follows:

1. First, to state the obvious, a mentor must have respect for the complicated nature of the institution or agency, and for everyone within that environment. He cannot represent the highest human values or the maximum potential of poetry if he is judgmental in this work.
2. He needs to be flexible and patient within an institutional or agency setting, always. He must coach his team of writing mentors to that same expectation.

3. He must communicate well within an institution or agency, being inclusive of institution staff in describing plans, making requests, and documenting accomplishments.

4. In preparing to work with youth, a writing mentor should plan a variety of activities and methods, so that he has alternatives and can adapt to that day's situation. For example, he might prepare an activity on a serious theme, such as "Regrets," but also have a lighter activity in which people describe their favorite foods, in case the group is troubled and unfocused. Also, he might bring a number of alternatives, in case the group burns through a lot of activities that day. A mentor might have some activities in which the group engages with one another, and other activities in which the group members work quietly on their own.

5. On the day of the writing session, a mentor must psychologically prepare himself so that he can be emotionally present for youth. He might pause to think through how he wants to be that day, before he walks through the institution door. He must bring energy and focus into the writing session to properly function with a vulnerable population that has complex needs and problems.

6. A mentor might go early to his scheduled activity, if possible, to check out the environment, fix problems, and adapt his plans.

7. A mentor should strategize with any colleagues so that they will help him engage with youth and deal with problems during an activity. A mentor's colleagues must be active participants in the process to help him.

8. A mentor should be very aware of transitions for the group, and communicate them clearly. For example, a mentor can make youth aware, up front, that he knows when the group will end, how it will end (e.g., that a particular staff person will escort the participants out), and about what will happen at each stage as he goes along. The mentor should then carefully hold to this schedule.

9. It is appropriate for a writing mentor to thank the group participants at the end.

15

Publishing Teen Poetry

Drugs
by a young woman, age 14

Because you never taught me that I was supposed to love myself.
Because you are jealous of me, your child, for every accomplishment I've fought for.
Because I want to show you that I am as low as you are. Then maybe we'd have something to talk about.
Because you abuse me with no shame.
Because self-mutilation has been glorified so many times by your lips. It is the only thing worthy of your attention.
Because you never expected any more of me.
Because I am definitely your child.
Because the people that you care about are the people that are more f***ed up than you.
Because I don't know how to heal the pain you bestowed upon me.
Because you never wanted me to amount to more than you are.
Because I am confused and young and you offer me no guidance.
Because you taught me how to.
Because I see how you don't have to care about anything while you're high.
Because I want to be just like you, Mother—painless, soulless.

Because maybe hurting myself will hurt you, too.
Because this is the way you planned it.
Because if I hit rock bottom, I don't have to fall in panic anymore.
Because I want you to love me.

It is a wonderful thing to value young writers, their words and lives, through publication. Pongo has published five hundred of its authors in thirteen books. But the significance of publication is much greater than the act of recognizing individual published authors.

With table displays at arts festivals, Pongo has used its publications as a way to talk with ten thousand people in the community about the poetry and lives of our authors. Five hundred people may visit Pongo in the course of a festival weekend. Everyone is asked to read a poem. Pongo's books have been honored with festival awards. One hundred people buy copies of Pongo's books in a weekend. Eighty people sign up to be on Pongo's mailing list.

Among the people who visit Pongo at these festivals are people who tell us their stories. Sometimes they share their stories for the first time. Adults with grown families talk about having been homeless or incarcerated as teens, having been abused as children. Parents tell painful stories of their children who are currently struggling with drugs. Parents come by the Pongo table with their children to talk. Homeless teens, current Pongo authors, will visit us.

Once I met a twenty-five-year-old young woman named Maggie, who was browsing Pongo's books at a festival. She was a graduate student and teacher, who looked up from the Pongo poetry and told me her difficult personal story, a story that she had hidden from the "good" people in her life. Maggie had been sexually abused to age seven by a stepbrother, neglected by a deeply disturbed mother in a squalid home, and kicked out of the house at thirteen, after which she lived under a bridge, became drug addicted, and involved herself with a violent boyfriend for many years. Yet Maggie always went to school and wrote poetry. When her brother admitted his guilt in the abuse, and Maggie was nineteen, she began her climb to heal herself. The opening poem of this chapter is from the period of Maggie's homelessness and drug use. It is addressed to her mother.

The Pongo books inspire openness, respect, and a celebration of all distressed youth.

Agencies and institutions have used Pongo books as a way of representing the youth they serve. They have given books to donors and made youth poetry the centerpiece of their fund-raisers.

Pongo has used its books to represent itself over the years, as a way of demonstrating our enduring commitment to the Pongo authors and our mission.

The most important benefit from the Pongo books is the significance of the poetry to other youth, other than the published authors. Pongo distributes its books for free to youth (as we make Pongo poetry available on our website). When distressed young people read poetry by their peers, they learn that they are not alone in their difficult experiences and strong feelings.

Pongo wants all of its writers, whether they are published or not, to know that they are part of the greater acknowledgment of Pongo poetry—that people who have had difficult lives have important things to say.

This chapter will discuss publication in terms of the legal/ethical issues (confidentiality, copyright, parental approvals, and remuneration) and the practical issues (timing, project scope, financing, and manuscript editing). Finally, it will share Pongo's Writer Release form, which enables Pongo to publish youth poetry.

Legal and Ethical Issues of Publishing

The sections below discuss book publishing in terms of confidentiality, copyrights, parental approval, and remuneration. Pongo's own ethical considerations are mentioned in the discussions. As should be evident, the issues of publication are complicated and necessitate good professional advice and good collaboration with any institution that hosts a writing project.

Confidentiality

Pongo's principal sites, juvenile detention and the state psychiatric hospital, require that Pongo preserve the young people's confidentiality in our publications. These sites do not want Pongo to use real names, even if we were to limit ourselves to first names. Pongo does invite its authors to suggest their own pseudonyms, but it's Pongo's usual practice to use arbitrary pseudonyms, for several reasons. It's often unclear if the names that youth provide are names by which they're commonly known in their communities. Also, sometimes youth request that Pongo use gang monikers, street names, or names that demean the youth.

In addition, Pongo has made the ethical decision to preserve teens' confidentiality even in situations where it is not required, even though some authors would like us to use their real names. The Pongo authors are young, with their whole lives ahead of them. Pongo wants these youth to have control over who knows about their difficult experiences. Also, families do change and reconcile. Pongo wants its authors to have every opportunity to reconcile with their families in the future. Finally, Pongo wants to protect its authors and itself from doing harm (by spreading incorrect information) or experiencing harm (by suffering someone's violent reaction to the teens' words).

Copyrights

Copyright is defined by law. Pongo has its own lawyer to advise it on these matters, and Pongo recommends that other organizations seek counsel. Our current understanding is that young writers own the poetry that they create, with copyright, and that they can legally give Pongo permission to publish that work. However, if youth make agreements when they are under eighteen, they have the right to change those agreements once they turn eighteen.

Pongo asks the youth to sign the Pongo Writer Release form, if they wish, to give Pongo permission to publish their work. Publication is always presented as a possibility, not a promise. Almost every youth signs this form, enthusiastically. The release form is discussed, below.

In its agreement with youth, Pongo does not ask for ownership of the teens' work. That would go against our principles of supporting the teens' voices. Sometimes there are others who want to publish the teens' work, but who require the youth to transfer ownership. Pongo opposes such arrangements.

Another aspect of the teens' ownership of their own poetry is that Pongo has no right to give permission to others (other magazines, books, or websites) to publish the teens' poetry, unless the youth themselves give us that permission. The Pongo Writer Release provides youth the opportunity to give us this permission at the time the poem is written. Pongo is frequently contacted by others who wish to republish our authors' writing.

Parental Approvals

Pongo's project sites have not required that Pongo obtain parental approvals in order to publish teen writing. Occasionally an outside organization wants to republish writing by Pongo's authors, but requests parental consent. It is often impractical to obtain this consent because of young people's complicated situations, including broken families, unknown family addresses, and changing guardianship. There is also the fact that teens may have mixed feelings about openly sharing poetry in which they discuss their family.

Sometimes therapists will want to bring Pongo youth poetry into family meetings (with a teen's permission), as a way of helping youth and family members connect with one another. There is a lot of sharing of youth poetry at the state psychiatric hospital, for example. Pongo works with youth and agencies to support this kind of dialogue.

Remuneration

People sometimes ask if Pongo authors are paid. Unfortunately, it would be impossible to distribute money equitably to teens. Most of the published authors could not be reached. Also, many worthy Pongo writers are not published. In addition, it would feel inappropriate to reward the occasional poetry that celebrates poor judgment or illegal activities.

So Pongo authors are not paid for their writing—but neither does Pongo itself profit from the teens' poetry. Pongo puts money from book sales back into the project, for example to pay for appearances at festivals. Pongo's principal use of its books is to give them away to youth. Pongo's principal intention with its books is to share its authors' important words with others.

Practical Issues of Publishing

Publishing can be a significant complement and support for the core work of facilitating personal creative expression by distressed youth, but there are several things to understand about publication. First, though it often arises as an afterthought, *publication is most easily achieved if it is planned for from the beginning of a writing project,* so that approvals can be gathered directly from the youth. Second, though it may feel like a sideline, *publication can require significant time and effort,* depending on the scope and aspirations of the publication. Third, though it may seem like a way to support a writing project, *publication is not a way to make money.* Fourth, though it may seem natural to "fix" teen writing with a rewrite, *publication requires a gentle touch on the part of an editor.*

The sections below discuss book publishing in terms of timing, project scope, financing, and manuscript editing.

Timing

Pongo highly recommends that writing projects consider the possibility of publication before they begin their work with youth. The best time to obtain a teen's approval for publication is at the time the youth writes, when the youth is sitting with a writing mentor and her work is in front of her. A writing project is well served if, in advance of working with youth, it has

- anticipated the possibility of publication in discussions with an agency,
- developed a Writer Release form, and
- organized a system for saving and cataloguing the teen writing and permission forms.

The main problem with considering publication as an afterthought is that it can be a significant challenge to reach teen authors after their time inside an institution. The teens' contact information goes out of date very quickly, if a person has legal access to it. There are additional ethical and practical problems with contacting youth outside an institution, when the youth may be shy, struggling, unsafe, or geographically dispersed.

On the other hand, it is true that some youth do appreciate the outreach from caring writing mentors. Pongo has sometimes reached youth through caseworkers and probation counselors, if the youth have only recently been discharged from the institution.

Project Scope

The options for printing have greatly increased, even in the time since Pongo published its last book. It's necessary to research to learn the range of output and cost. The publishing choices include printing technique, quantity, length, dimensions, paper choice, whether to include art, whether to use color (inside and/or on the cover), and binding.

In the past, Pongo's books have been professionally printed (offset printing), in quantities of 1,500 to 3,000 copies, but have used volunteer editors and book designers. Pongo's early books were in chapbook form, about sixty-four pages in length (front matter plus poetry), 6" x 9" in dimensions, using no art, with black ink only, and with staples in the center. More recently Pongo's published books have been "perfect bound" (had spines) with full-color covers.

Financing

In Pongo's experience the income from book sales is very small, and it can require time to monitor consignment sales or to ship Internet sales. Pongo recommends that people have low expectations from book sales. Pongo's preference for financing is to apply for grants that pay for printing and that allow Pongo to give books away, where it can achieve great good in the community.

Manuscript Editing

The role of an editor is *not* to change a teen's poem so that it becomes the poem the editor would have written. The editor's role calls for restraint. Pongo places priority on the teens' personal voices, including idiomatic language. The appropriate guidelines for the editor are that she remove misspellings, make grammar consistent, and clarify references so that errors do not detract from the author's intention. There may be additional decisions, for clarity, in placement of line breaks and spacing between stanzas.

(In contrast to this restraint, there is the fact the Pongo writing mentor may collaborate with a youth at the time a poem is written, offering lots of ideas and suggestions. But the particular quality of the mentor's input at that time is that she is listening to the author, offering suggestions in the moment, and confirming that the mentor's ideas suit the writer's voice and intention.)

There is another role for an editor, at the time of publication, when the editor must not only check the Writer Release form and assign a pseudonym, but change any significant detail in a teen's poem that might identify the youth. This detail might include the breed and name of a pet, the names of siblings, the place of origin, etc.

Pongo's Writer Release Form

Figure 15.1 contains Pongo's Writer Release form, which incorporates Pongo's response to the legal, ethical, and practical considerations of publishing. The second page of the form is Pongo's Author Survey form. The Writer Release and Survey are handed to a writer to sign, if he wishes, at the end of a writing session. Almost every poet eagerly signs the form. The signed form is then stapled to the front of a hard copy of the author's writing from that day. The form and writing are filed, by author first name, in a binder for that project year. The Microsoft Word file of the poem itself is named, using the author's first name, the first three letters of her last name, the date, a number (if multiple poems were written that day), and the mentor's initials. The files are all saved in a directory for that project year.

Pongo Teen Writing: Writer's Release

Name (please print clearly): _____

Date of birth (month, day, and year): _____

Contact address, email, and phone (if available): _____

_____

_____

I understand that my participation in the Pongo Publishing writing and publishing project is entirely voluntary. I understand that Richard Gold's publications and readings will help me express myself to an audience of sympathetic readers.

I certify that the writing I give to Richard Gold is my original work. I give permission to Richard Gold to use my writing in his publications, print or electronic, and to read or perform my writing as well. I also give permission to Richard Gold to use my writing in the creation and publication of activities for other writers.

I understand that I still own my writing and have the right to use or sell my work in any way that I want. I also understand that if Richard Gold's publications, readings, and activities make any money, that money will not go to me or to Richard Gold but will be used to provide free poetry books to teenagers or to support charities that help teenagers.

I understand that Richard Gold may make changes to my writing in order to protect my privacy and that of others. I understand that Richard Gold will not use my real name or initials in his publications, although he may include my real age and gender. I understand that Richard will choose another name for me, but I may indicate my preference, below:

    My preferred other name is _____.

I understand that Richard Gold's publications may include my dedication, if I want one.

    Please dedicate my writing to _____.

I understand that Richard Gold has occasional opportunities to submit teen writing to magazines, web sites, exhibits, competitions, anthologies, etc. If I choose to check the box below, I give Richard Gold permission to submit my work to these forums under my alias. I understand that Richard Gold will do his best to notify me of any recognition or award I receive. I understand that these forums rarely offer payment.

    ❏ I give permission to submit my writing to magazines, web sites, exhibits, etc.

Signature _____Date_____

FIGURE 15.1
Pongo's Writer Release Form and Author Survey

Pongo Teen Writing: Author Survey

Dear Author,

Thank you for sharing your writing with the Pongo Teen Writing Project! Please complete this quick, optional survey about how the writing went for you.

1. Did you enjoy this writing experience?
    Yes_____   No_____

2. How much writing have you done before working with Pongo?
    A lot_____   Some_____   A little_____   None_____

3. Do you feel proud of the writing you did with us?
    Yes_____   No_____

4. Did you write about things that you don't normally talk about?
    Yes_____   No_____

5. Do you feel that you learned something about writing?
    Yes_____   No_____

6. Do you feel that you learned something about yourself?
    Yes_____   No_____

7. If you wrote about things that are bothering you, did the writing help you feel better?
    Yes_____   No_____

8. Do you think you might write more in the future?
    Yes_____   No_____

9. If so, do you think you might write during times when life is difficult?
    Yes_____   No_____

10. Is there anything we can do to make the writing experience better for you?
    _____

11. Is there anything else you'd like to say about the writing experience?
    _____

FIGURE 15.1
(*continued*)

Epilogue: Next Steps

How I Feel Today
by a young man in the state psychiatric hospital, age 14

I can't really grasp it, my feeling
I feel Weird, like a monkey skateboarding on a banana
I'm the monkey
I'm skateboarding on the banana because I just got out of school
So we were cooking with giant bananas
So, I decided to dehydrate this banana so I could skateboard
On this banana chip
With a Blue, red, black, and yellow helmet on his knee
The helmet is on my knee because I think it's the new style
It's what monkeys wear in Paris
I like the helmet because I like lightning
The helmet reminds me of lightning
I feel Confused, like a young girl walking through a store
And seeing Water Chestnuts And not knowing what they are
I feel Jittery, like a business man at a meeting
With four cups of coffee and two four-hour energies
With seventeen energy drinks in his body
I like energy drinks
The man likes energy drinks, too

Teachers and counselors, you have my respect and best wishes. You're at the conclusion of this book, *Writing with At-Risk Youth: The Pongo Teen Writing Method*. We've covered a lot of ground together. How do you feel about making a start with teaching personal poetry to the young people in your care? Do you feel eager and excited? Do you feel a little hesitant, possibly unsure of yourself? Do you wonder how to begin? Do you wonder if you will succeed?

In this epilogue I discuss some of the feelings in this work. I present some simple things that you can do tomorrow to make a beginning. I also offer some ways that Pongo can help, through our website, phone consultation, and a community of other writing mentors.

The World of Emotion

Expressive writing is easy because of the power of our emotional lives. Expressive writing is challenging for the same reason. Emotions are a common and natural language between people, but often an ambivalent one. Suppose a person's parent died recently. Suppose that person was hurt by her parent. Suppose that person doesn't want to be angry. Suppose that person is holding a lot of complicated and unarticulated feelings inside. It can be a frightening thing to consider writing poetry.

The Pongo Teen Writing Method shows that distressed young people will express the emotions they need to express, through poetry, if they are given an attentive ear and a supportive creative opportunity without pressure or expectation. When these youth write, they often experience very sad feelings, but also feel considerable pride and relief afterward.

But how do we feel, as the young people's teachers and counselors, about accessing some of our own emotions in the process of working with youth? Suppose the teacher is the person who lost a parent recently? How does she feel about teaching poetry as the language of emotional truth?

As teachers and counselors using the Pongo Teen Writing Method, our openness to our own difficult emotions may be our first challenge, but also a great opportunity. Emotions may arise in us, and we will need to be aware of them, though there is no pressure to express them when it doesn't feel right.

Sometimes, by entering the world of emotion in poetry, we might find relief for ourselves, along with the youth.

It can be a brave thing to be a teacher of writing, as it can be a brave thing to be a distressed youth who writes.

I believe in this process. I believe in you.

Next Steps

In terms of designing a writing program for youth, it's important to understand that you can begin modestly. For example, if you are new to working with distressed young people, you don't need to begin by starting your own writing program. You can begin by volunteering inside an institution, with an experienced teacher, where you have the opportunity to meet the teens.

If you are a teacher or counselor who is new to teaching poetry, you don't need to begin by planning an entire poetry unit. You can begin by sharing poems with your class, talking about poems, inviting youth to create their own poems, and saving their work. You can find poems on the Pongo website to share.

If you want to go further, you can use the Pongo fill-in-the-blank writing activities with the youth in your care. These activities are easy to use and effective. You can find and download them from the Pongo site.

The one thing you need to do, in making a beginning, is to have an open and accepting attitude toward the young people's words and experiences. You need to be a listener. You can ask the youth to "Write from the heart about who you are." You can give them an opportunity to share their work with their peers.

To help yourself, you can look for colleagues with whom you can share this experience, colleagues with whom you can plan and talk along the way. You can also contact Pongo, as explained below.

How Pongo Can Help

Pongo has resources for you on its website, www.pongoteenwriting.org. In addition to poetry and writing activities, there is teaching information and a blog.

Pongo offers one-day trainings in Seattle, and it also offers workshops at agencies and conferences. These are discussed on the website. You can write to us.

Pongo supports new writing projects on the Pongo model. Pongo calls them "duckling" projects. These projects are located in different states, at sites that include detention centers, homeless shelters, and psychiatric hospitals. Pongo will confer with you if you want to start a duckling project. For example, Pongo can advise you on how to talk to agencies, how to find volunteers, and how to plan for publishing. Pongo can coach you further in applying the Pongo Teen Writing Method.

You are welcome to e-mail Pongo for advice and to set up a free phone consultation. Pongo mentors are available to help. There is a Pongo community that includes the current duckling projects.

Teachers and counselors, you have Pongo's support. From its inception, the Pongo Teen Writing Method has had unanticipated therapeutic effects for youth and unanticipated growth opportunities for the teachers and counselors who adopt it. Nothing could please us more than to share these experiences with your students and you. Feel free to call on Pongo Teen Writing.

References

Davies, Jody M., and Mary G. Frawley. 1994. *Treating the Adult Survivor of Childhood Sexual Abuse: A Psychoanalytic Perspective.* New York: Basic Books.

Herman, Judith L. 1997. *Trauma and Recovery.* New York: Basic Books.

Kalsched, Donald. 2001. *The Inner World of Trauma: Archetypal Defenses of the Personal Spirit.* New York: Brunner-Routledge.

Karen, Robert. 1998. *Becoming Attached: First Relationships and How They Shape Our Capacity to Love.* New York: Oxford University Press.

Koch, Kenneth. 1971. *Wishes, Lies, and Dreams.* New York: Vintage.

Luka, Miral. 2006. "Pongo Study: Summary of Findings." Unpublished report.

Rynearson, Edward K. 2001. *Retelling Violent Death.* Philadelphia: Brunner-Routledge.

Rynearson, Edward K., Jennifer Favell, Vicki Belluomini, Richard Gold, and Holly Prigerson. 2006. "Restorative Retelling with Incarcerated Juveniles." In *Violent Death: Resilience and Intervention beyond the Crisis,* edited by Edward K. Rynearson, pp. 275–91. New York: Routledge.

Schultz, Rosalyn. 1990. "Secrets of Adolescence: Incest and Developmental Fixations." In *Incest-Related Syndromes of Adult Psychopathology,* edited by Richard P. Kluft, pp. 133–59. Washington, DC: American Psychiatric Press.

Steiner, Hans, Ivan G. Garcia, and Zakee Matthews. 1997. "Post-Traumatic Stress Disorder in Incarcerated Juvenile Delinquents." *Journal of the American Academy of Child and Adolescent Psychiatry*, 36(3): 357–65.

van der Kolk, Bessel A. 2007a. "The Body Keeps the Score: Approaches to the Psychobiology of Traumatic Stress Disorder." In *Traumatic Stress: The Effects of Overwhelming Experience on Mind, Body, and Society*, edited by Bessel A. van der Kolk, Alexander C. McFarlane, and Lars Weisaeth, pp. 214–41. New York: Guilford Publications.

———. 2007b. "The Complexity of Adaptation to Trauma: Self-Regulation, Stimulus, and Characterological Development." In *Traumatic Stress: The Effects of Overwhelming Experience on Mind, Body, and Society*, edited by Bessel A. van der Kolk, Alexander C. McFarlane, and Lars Weisaeth, pp. 182–213. New York: Guilford Publications.

———. 2007c. "Trauma and Memory." In *Traumatic Stress: The Effects of Overwhelming Experience on Mind, Body, and Society*, edited by Bessel A. van der Kolk, Alexander C. McFarlane, and Lars Weisaeth, pp. 279–302. New York: Guilford Publications.

About the Author

Richard Gold, MA, of Seattle founded the Pongo Teen Writing Project, a nonprofit that offers unique therapeutic poetry programs to adolescents who are homeless, in jail, or in other ways leading difficult lives. In its seventeen years, Pongo has worked with over six thousand teens. The Pongo website contains writing activities for distressed youth and resources for teachers: www.pongoteenwriting.org. Prior to founding Pongo, Richard was managing editor of Microsoft Press. In 2010, Richard was named a Microsoft Integral Fellow, honored for his work with Pongo, by Bill and Melinda Gates and the Microsoft Alumni Foundation. A book of Richard's illustrated poetry, *The Odd Puppet Odyssey,* was published in 2003. In this book, the character Pongo is a puppet who struggles awkwardly with becoming human, until he aspires to compassion.